From The Heart of Europe to The Pacific Northwest

To Teddy

with love

Jacli

December 2007

From The Heart of Europe to The Pacific Northwest

✦

A Memoir of the 20th Century

Dorli Mason

iUniverse, Inc.

New York Lincoln Shanghai

From The Heart of Europe to The Pacific Northwest
A Memoir of the 20th Century

iUniverse books may be ordered through booksellers or by contacting:

iUniverse
2021 Pine Lake Road, Suite 100
Lincoln, NE 68512
www.iuniverse.com
1-800-Authors (1-800-288-4677)

Because of the dynamic nature of the Internet, any Web addresses or links contained in this book may have changed since publication and may no longer be valid.

The views expressed in this work are solely those of the author and do not necessarily reflect the views of the publisher, and the publisher hereby disclaims any responsibility for them.

ISBN: 978-0-595-43276-9 (pbk)
ISBN: 978-0-595-87617-4 (ebk)

Printed in the United States of America

To my grandchildren, Andrew and Claire

Acknowledgement

Without the existence of i-Universe, my grandchildren would never have had access to more than a heap of typewritten pages.

In addition, these pages would never have become a book without the help of my friend, Jane Meyer Brahm, who spent many hours as my "editor" arranging my written thoughts into what became a publishable manuscript.

My heartfelt thanks go to Jane Meyer Brahm and to i-Universe for their help and advice along the way.

Contents

Writing about my life has been on my mind for some time. The 20th century was, after all, a very turbulent one and pretty soon there will be few of us alive who have lived through some of it.

Inspired by the start of the new millennium I sat down at my computer in February, 2000 and began to write.

I realized very quickly, however, that I would have to rely almost exclusively on memory. My older sister, Marietta Freeman-Attwood, died almost two years ago, my younger sister, Christine von Cavallar, is very ill in Vienna, and few documents were part of my parents' exodus from Czechoslovakia in 1948.

Early Childhood Years

As I start with my birth on June 16, 1926 in Altenberg, Czechoslovakia, my memory kicks in with the story that may or may not be based on fact. After the birth of my older sister Marietta in 1923, my mother had a miscarriage and when pregnant again with me, did not want to take any chances of losing the baby. She consulted an eminent specialist in Vienna, who agreed to travel to Altenberg when the time came. According to family legend, he arrived in early June with a nurse who was also a midwife, and settled in to await the birth.

Early June is asparagus time in southern Czechoslovakia and we grew the coveted white kind. The Herr Professor was very impressed with our cuisine, especially the way the cook prepared asparagus, and was fed it every day for lunch. My father, with impeccable manners, suffered through these lunches when the Herr Professor regaled him with gruesome tales of difficult deliveries.

On the day of my birth, so the story goes, the doctor was again eating his favorite vegetable when the nurse appeared to inform him that the birth had started.

"Delay the birth. I must finish my asparagus first!" the doctor is said to have uttered. I was born without his assistance upstairs. Needless to say, my younger sister was born two years later in the local hospital. The threat to call me "Asparagus" was also not carried out. I was named "Theodora Maria Ernestine Wilhelmine." Theodora after my mother's father Theodor Kern, Ernestine after my mother, and Wilhelmine after my father's first name.

The "Villa," as our house was called in the village, had been built either by my maternal great-great-grandfather, Enoch Kern, or by his son Berthold, father of Theodor, my grandfather, in the early part of the 19th century. It was a large house consisting of two floors where the family lived and one floor "below stairs" for the servants' quarters, kitchens, laundry facilities and wine cellars. A "dumb-waiter" brought the food from the kitchen to the first floor. A wide corridor ran the length of each floor, and a marble staircase with the obligatory red carpet covering the stairs connected the lower and upper floor. All rooms opened onto the corridors. One had to cross the hallway to get to the bathrooms and toilets—always separate rooms—and in the winter, during the night, in order to avoid crossing the ice-cold corridor, everyone relied on chamber pots in their bedrooms.

Each bedroom was also equipped with a washstand and a portable bidet, all nicely hidden behind screens. A large terrace ran the length of the lower floor with some of the rooms opening onto the terrace through French windows. The salon was connected to a heated glassed-in winter garden, full of beautiful and exotic plants. This winter garden curved down onto a glass house below, where wood was stored and plants were grown in flats.

The terrace had a staircase that took you down into the garden. In other words, you entered the house at street level, but the garden, more park than garden, was on a lower level. By the time I grew up, the park had large trees and extended all the way to the river "Iglava," giving us complete privacy. The terrace had a large sunroof which could be wheeled out for shade. We lived on the terrace in summer—we ate breakfast in an arbor, overgrown with ivy, had afternoon tea and relaxed in lounge-chairs.

If one continued on the road past the Villa, one came to the "Fabrik," the factory that my maternal great-grandfather or maybe even his father, Enoch Kern, had built. It was a factory that made fine wool cloth and in its day it was one of the largest in the old Austro-Hungarian Empire. It was also the source of great wealth for my mother's family in the days before World War I. My grandfather, Theodor Kern, had loaned large amounts of money in gold value to the Emperor of Austria. With the end of the Empire after World War I and the creation of Czechoslovakia as an independent state, these loans were never paid back. My grandfather died shortly after the end of World War I, with no one ready to step into his shoes and by the mid-1930s, the factory had to be sold and that source of wealth ceased to fuel the lifestyle of my family. My early childhood memories are of servants, of gardeners, of nannies and governesses and grand parties that my parents gave—only to be replaced by genteel poverty in my teens and during World War II.

My father, Wilhelm Cavallar von Grabensprung, who had been a professional soldier during World War I, met my mother at a party and, as he used to tell us, "fell in love with her beautiful hands, even before he fell in love with her." Ernestine, or "Stenny" as she was known, was the second daughter of Theodor Kern and Heda (nee Koppen von Hessenwalde). They were married in 1921 and had three girls, Marietta, born in 1923; Theodora or Dorli as I was called, in 1926; and Christine in 1928. They were a beautiful couple, both very good looking, my mother gentle and motherly but with a sense of humor that kept life very much in perspective; my father with the courtly manners of a 19th century gentleman and an old-fashioned sense of honor that made him a beloved figure not only among his friends, but in the village and among his employees as well.

My father had been a great World War I hero, earning the highest decoration that the Empire had to give in times of war, the Maria Theresian Cross. This medal was no ordinary medal given for bravery in the face of the enemy. Empress Maria Theresa had created it during her reign and stipulated that it could only be awarded for "an act of valor and personal initiative on the battlefield that had significant impact on the battle itself." The medal was always awarded by the emperor (or empress) in person. The recipient of the medal would be asked what he would like to do with his life after the War, and if possible, that wish would be granted. My father's wish had been to become commander of his alma mater, the military academy Wienerneustadt, the equivalent of West Point in the U.S.A. Unfortunately, the collapse of the Empire made this a moot point. Upon the death of the recipient, the medal had to be returned to the order of the Maria Theresia Cross, to be awarded again in a subsequent war. It was only because the Empire ceased to exist after World War I that my father had been allowed to keep the medal.

One other royal decree went with the award of the medal. The recipient was knighted, or, if he already had a title, was given the next higher title. Thus my father became a baron by royal decree. After my father's death, the family gave the medal to the Austrian Heeresmuseum in Vienna, where it can still be viewed in a glass case.

My father earned his medal as a young lieutenant on the Eastern front where, while on patrol with a dozen men, he came upon a bridgehead the Serbs had established on the Austrian side of the river Save. After overwhelming the enemy at the bridgehead he forced one of their gunners to turn a captured gun around and shoot at the bridge. With the help of one of his own men he then activated the rest of the captured guns and within a short time had damaged the bridge so severely that the advance of a whole division of Serbs was halted, thrown into total confusion, which in turn led to their destruction. He was severely wounded in the encounter, had been given "last rites" and was not expected to live. But when he was informed of the award by his brother in the hospital, he decided to live—and he did.

After marriage to my mother, my father joined the directors in my grandfather's factory to try to keep it running in the new environment of Czechoslovakia, the independent country that emerged from the ashes of World War I. My father, alas, had no training as a businessman and eventually the factory passed into other hands. He then turned to supervising the running of our farm and a small brick-making factory that he had bought. In years to come my mother sold some of her jewelry to help make ends meet.

But essentially, life went on as before. There were fewer servants, but we still had Rosi, the cook, and her husband, Anton, the butler/house man. They had more or less grown up within the family and stayed with my parents all through the Russian occupation. A chambermaid came daily from the village, as did weekly washer women and women who cleaned. My grandmother's personal maid, Maria Kuplien, also had become a member of the household and been with us for decades. Euli, our governess, came when Christine and I were about five and three years old. She stayed with us for almost 10 years, until she married the local blacksmith. Her only son, Washku, was delivered one stormy winter night by my mother when transport to the hospital was impossible. Euli (her real name was Bertha) was a friend and a brick in times of need. Christine and I visited her in an old-age home in Iglau in 1994 when she was in her 90s—still spry and full of good cheer.

The Four Seasons

Life in Altenberg was geared to the seasons.

Spring

Spring always meant BIG house cleaning. All the rugs were dragged onto the lawn and vigorously beaten with bamboo instruments that looked like tennis racquets, only with bamboo lattice works instead of strings. All winter clothing and car blankets were hung outside and brushed and inspected for spots that had to be cleaned before everything was put into cloth bags and stored away. Mothballs were stuffed and sprinkled onto everything. The whole house smelled of mothballs for weeks afterwards.

A group of men from the village came to polish the parquet floors. They would apply wax to the floors and then polish by wearing brushes on their feet and rhythmically sliding to and fro across the floor. Windows were washed, the terrace swept and the terrace furniture washed and set up for the summer. The earthenware urns along the terrace balustrade were filled with geraniums and seedlings went into flower beds. Two gardeners were in charge of the vegetable garden, pruning fruit trees and preparing the beds for planting. We took long walks into the woods, looking for primulas, violets and daffodils and counting the returning song birds.

Summer

Summer was a time of leisure, of wide open windows and breakfast on the terrace.

We went swimming in the river, upstream from the factory, where the water was clean. We took long walks after tea and before dinner, sometimes just Euli and we children, but often my parents as well. We loved it when my mother was along, as she always could be persuaded to tell stories, stories that she made up as she went along and that were much more exciting than the stories in our books.

As we got older, we used to sit after dinner on the terrace, playing games such as "When I was a slave in Troy, watching from the ramparts the advance of Agamemnon's army...." Someone had to pick up from there and after a while pass it on to someone else. The stories had to be clever, historically correct and very often were very funny. If you did not measure up, you were declared OUT.

We watched the stars in the sky and learned to identify them. Summer was also the time when the house was full of guests and friends, but mostly family—my mother's sisters with their families and her brother, Hans, usually accompanied by one of his beautiful mistresses. The table in the dining room would be fully extended, seating up to 24 persons for lunch, which was always the big meal of the day.

Our tennis court was in full use, with my father regularly winning as he was by far the best player. Onkel Hans produced films for a living, and to amuse himself he sometimes wrote and produced a play based on the residents of the house. The play was always funny, though at times a bit unkind to one or another person. We all had roles and rehearsed for days on end. The premiere, to which we invited friends, was the highlight of the summer.

Fall

Fall meant harvest and hunting parties. From the age of 12 or 13 on, we were encouraged to help the village farmers with their harvest. On the high plateau of Iglau, the farmers grew poppy seeds (most of the meals in Czechoslovakia include a dish or two that requires the use of poppy seeds). They grew rye, wheat and barley and endless acres of potatoes. At noon, the farmer's wife would bring lunch. Each person received a hunk of bread into which a hole had been dug and filled with butter or "schmalz" (pork fat). The men drank beer. We children drank cool milk from metal drinking cups. Salt was passed around to sprinkle on the butter or schmalz. We loved it! The lunch made up for the hard work.

Much less pleasant was the picking of potatoes. Schools made students available for potato picking, a duty we dreaded. It was cold and backbreaking work. We picked the potatoes by hand, collected them into baskets which were then emptied into horse-drawn wagons. (During World War II we were assigned to do this work for days on end, sometimes under very harsh weather conditions.)

After the vast fields had been harvested, the hunting season started. I loved to walk the fields with my father looking for partridge or pheasant. We would usually come home with at least one brace of birds.

Winter

Winters in Czechoslovakia were cold and snowy. The rooms in the house were heated with individual coal (or wood) stoves. Because the ceilings were extremely high, and heat rises, we never were really warm. There were drafts and to cross the corridor to go to the bathroom was an effort usually left to the last minute. My father had a heater put into one of the toilets as he liked to peruse the local paper while seated on the throne. We children were usually not allowed to use HIS bathroom. In the "winter" living room—in contrast to the salon which was only heated during the Christmas season—my mother sat in her favorite chair with her feet on a cushion against drafts and after lunch she would recline on a sofa, covered with a fur blanket and slowly eat some of the very special chocolates she imported from Hungary.

The fun of winter was definitely the abundance of snow. We would visit other houses in horse-drawn sleds. The adults sat wrapped in fur blankets in the sleds, while we children were pulled behind on skis or sleds. We built huge snowmen and had skating parties on our pond. I still remember the delicious taste of hot chocolate that Euli provided out of large thermos bottles.

Looking back on Education

I do not remember much about early schooling. We may have been tutored at home for awhile, but it certainly did not leave a lasting impression. I do remember somewhere along the line the one-room elementary school in the village. I remember the teacher (not just from surviving photographs), a gentleman with a moustache whom I rather liked. I believe that grades 1 through 5 were all in one room.

Besides learning how to read and write and do elementary arithmetic, I remember gazing in fascination at the girl in front of me. All of us girls had pigtails, with a neat dividing line down the back of our heads. Her line was like a busy street with lice running up and down. It was not long before I had lice too, which were treated by soaking my hair in a solution of petroleum. My head was then wrapped into a towel and I had to bear the terrible burning sensation for 30 minutes or so, after which my hair was washed and the lice were presumed to be dead. Then Euli would comb my hair with a "lice-comb" for hours on end to take out the eggs.

After I was infested with lice a second time, I cut off one of my pigtails in frustration, only to regret it, and refuse to have the other one cut off. Eventually this must have been done, as pictures of me from a certain point on survive showing me with very short hair.

After finishing primary school in Altenberg I took the exam to enter Gymnasium, which was located in Iglau. One went to the Gymnasium (or to a trade school for which one did not have to take an entrance exam) for eight years and then took an exam called the "Matura." If you passed, you were entitled to enter University.

Going to school in Iglau was quite a change from the village school in Altenberg. Iglau was 3 km from Altenberg, a good walk of one hour or more each way. In the summer we could ride our bicycles, and before the war started we were taken by car to school, at least in the winter.

But mostly we biked or walked, which made for a very long day. The trek to and from school in the winter was miserably cold and accounted for chilblains at one time or other. During exam time we stayed with my great-aunt who had a house in Iglau. She had a very good cook, who spoiled us outrageously. We must have been good students, for I do not remember any school crisis or private tutoring to bring us up to par.

The war ended my Gymnasium education after four years. I was able to prolong school for two more years by entering a school that taught cooking and sewing, which were considered worthy of a German woman's education. After that I was caught up in war duties.

Wonderful Christmas memories

Preparations for Christmas started early in December. The whole house smelled of baking cookies, of cinnamon and melting chocolate, of spun sugar and homemade marzipan. We children were allowed to help cut out favorite forms on the enormous wooden board that covered a whole kitchen table. We put raisin faces on Lebkuchen men and women, used candied fruit to put "jewels" on cookie hearts, mushrooms and Christmas trees. We rolled rum balls in minced nuts and used little brushes to put icing on different cookies. The finished product was put on trays and into metal boxes and stored in our pantry, an unheated room adjacent to the kitchen which served as a place of refrigeration. Enormous quantities of Christmas cookies and Christmas bread were thus produced in the weeks before Christmas.

In the Christmas tradition of my childhood, Santa Claus did not slide down the chimney to bring the presents.

St. Nicholas came on December 6 to collect the list of wishes from the children and to remind them to "be good, obey their parents and generally behave like angels." Nikkolo, as he was known, looked more like a bishop than the jolly, bearded U.S. version. He carried a staff and wore a miter and was VERY dignified. He was accompanied by the devil, which lurked behind the door and made terrifying noises. The latter served to remind the children to REALLY mind St. Nicholas' words of admonition, otherwise only a "sack of coals" might be found under the Christmas tree.

It was the Christmas child who brought the presents. If you were lucky, you might see him fly by briefly and since he only could be seen at night, this took a lot of imagination. Sometimes the Christmas child left some angel hair to be found—that really meant he had been around your house.

In my childhood memories, there were no strings of light decorating trees or houses and no Santa on the roof top, riding in a sled pulled by reindeer. In my memory, Christmas was always associated with snow, deep soft blankets of snow that created a stillness around house and garden and village, as though the whole world was waiting for the big moment when Christ would be born.

On the afternoon of Christmas Eve my sisters and I would bring Christmas gifts to families of our choice. It had to be a poor family, one that could not afford much. We had prepared for weeks for this moment, had spent our allowance on things we bought and been given items by our parents that they thought would be welcome.

I remember agonizing at the local store where different candies were displayed in huge glass jars, over the type of candy I would buy. I usually settled on rock candy, those hunks of crystallized sugar, probably because they were my favorites. We were allowed to buy one toy for each child in our chosen family and were encouraged to add toys we owned, provided they were in good condition. We were allowed a box of Christmas cookies per family and always begged the cook for more—and we each decorated a small tree complete with candles.

We then loaded our sleds with these gifts and set off for the village, very much aware that we were about to bring joy to our selected family.

The one family that sticks in my mind, were the Stepniczkas—they lived in a damp, dark apartment by the river. Mrs. Stepniczka sewed for my mother—she did fine embroidery, initials on handkerchiefs and napkins. She would sit by the window in the gloomy afternoon light, trying to sew till there was no daylight left. I remember the smell of the apartment, a combination of raw onions and unwashed bodies. I hated the smell but forced myself to cheerfully embrace everyone and start unpacking the bounty from my sled.

Looking back, I realize that we exercised a very feudal custom: the children from the big house bringing Christmas to the poor. I also remember, however, how very touched I was by their joy.

It set the tone for our own Christmas. Euli, our governess, would talk to us on the way back about how lucky we were and how important it was to always remember those less fortunate.

We would arrive back home in time to check on the large carp we were to have for dinner which had been fished out of our pond and was swimming in the bathtub: an ugly fish, but part of the Christmas ritual.

The big salon had been locked for weeks. We knew that a large Christmas tree was being decorated by our parents with the help of the Christmas Child, but we did not see the tree until the doors opened on Christmas Eve.

With mounting excitement we changed into our best party frocks and assembled in the library to wait for the big moment. My grandmother read Christmas stories to us until we heard the tune of "Stille Nacht, Heilige Nacht" emanating from the old phonograph. The big doors to the salon opened and there stood our parents—my mother in a long evening gown and my father in black tie, and past them, in the depth of the room, stood the large tree ablaze with white candles and throughout the room were long tables covered with white linen that displayed the presents, one table for each child, for my parents, grandmother and Euli and the servants.

I always thought, as I looked into the room, that I could see Saint Peter himself, standing behind the tree, but when the electric lights were turned on, it was only Anton, our house man with a long stick ending in a wet sponge watching the lighted candles.

Even before I looked at my presents, I would look at the tree and mark the places where I could see the marzipan candy—a favorite of all three of us, and something we all wanted to get at early. Our Christmas tree had lots of candy hanging on it, and for once, we were allowed to pick at will.

The presents on the tables were not wrapped as they are here, so one could immediately find what one had hoped for most.

After wishing everyone a Merry Christmas, the family retreated to the dining room for the usual Christmas dinner of fish, a very fancy potato salad, a green salad and for desert a homemade pear and black cherry compote with an assortment of Christmas cookies.

But one more ritual had to be followed. Since my mother's childhood, someone had always faked choking on a fish-bone, with my grandmother having slight hysterics of "Jesu Maria and Josef, someone bring the child bread to chew before (he or) she chokes!!!!"

By the time we grew up, the one chosen to "choke" on Christmas Eve would practice how to choke convincingly and, depending on one's conception of mayhem, fall choking under the table or pretend to throw up. My grandmother dutifully reacted, although I am sure she no longer believed anything was really amiss. (Thank goodness no one ever really choked on a fish bone, as a carp is full of them).

The rest of the evening, we played with our toys, read our books and ate too much candy.

On Christmas Day, weather permitting, we went to Iglau, the next town, to attend church.

At mid-day we ate an enormous Christmas meal of homemade goose-liver pate, roast goose with red cabbage and dumplings, and for dessert, chestnut puree with whipped cream. It was a very heavy meal that had to be followed by some outdoor activity for us children and a nap for our parents.

The January Pig Feast

Around the middle of January a slaughtered pig, all pink and washed clean, would arrive by sled from our farm to be transformed into hams, pork roasts, chops, liver and blood sausages and vast amounts of lard.

Two butchers who were hired to accomplish this transformation were assisted by about 10 women from the village, all hired for this special occasion. The women were given white coats by my mother and had handkerchiefs to cover their hair. The large ironing room on the floor of the storage rooms and servant quarters was temporarily transformed into a "pig factory." The long tables were scrubbed clean and the job of the women consisted mostly of cutting up the fat of the pig into small squares. The fat was then cooked in huge vats, the liquid fat poured into earthenware crocks, to be used for cooking the rest of the year. The residue, the "grammeln," cooked till golden yellow and crisp, were a delicacy eaten with a bit of the fat on rye bread and enjoyed by everyone for months to come.

The job of the butchers was to cut up the meat into roasts, chops and hams to be cured and smoked. The intestines were washed and filled with sausage meat—every 12 centimeters, the filled roll was bound and cut, thus creating individual sausages.

My mother, with her World War I nurses' aid kit, would wander among the local women, bandaging cut fingers and making sure that strict cleanliness was observed.

The production lasted all day and was followed with great interest by us children.

On the first night, the pig's head, feet and tail were served boiled. It is the tenderest meat of all and considered a great delicacy.

Most of my parents' dinner parties were held during January. The whole countryside waited for an invitation to a pig feast.

Laundry Day

Actually, the laundry day was spread over several days: washing day, drying day and ironing day. All were exciting events of my early childhood. Several women from the village arrived early in the morning to begin sorting all items according to my mother's directions.

This took place "below stairs" in a huge room where large tubs were ready to be filled with hot soapy water. All items were presoaked first. The bed linen and towels were then boiled in a special vat where one woman would constantly stir them with a long wooden stick. All other garments were scrubbed on washboards. Each woman had a big bar of soap which she would work into the garments. I don't remember where and how the laundry was rinsed but a simple, hand-operated machine was used to press all water out of the washed items, which were then ready to be hung up to dry. In the summer, the drying was done outside; in the winter everything was hung on lines in the room with the wash tubs.

I loved "ironing" day best. At least five or six women were lined up at tables covered with flannel sheets to provide softness and stands for the irons. The irons had wooden handles which could be unclipped while the iron was being heated on top of a stove. One woman was in charge of constantly changing cooling irons for the workers. These ladies were experts—table linens and napkins were ironed and folded with great precision. Bed linen and pillow cases were folded in a precise pattern, always showing monograms off to advantage. The finished pieces were put into baskets and whisked upstairs to be sorted and put away into their proper places.

I remember sitting under one of the ironing tables, inhaling that sweet smell of clean laundry being ironed and listening to the women sing while rhythmically moving their irons across the ironing board. They would sing of love and betrayal, of cowardice and heroism, and of life and death.

I still remember snatches of their songs: "Rinaldini, the girl whispered, Rinaldini wake up—the sun has risen blood red in the East and your men are ready to fight and die...." or: "Johann Sebastian Seidelbast hanged himself from a branch—("Ast"—in German which rhymes with Seidelbast) stuck out his tongue and blew out his last breath. He had forsaken his love and she had thrown herself under a train—she died and with a last whimper; so did the baby she was carrying...."

All these songs were very dramatic and mostly sad and quite unsuitable for a small child to be listening to—which made hiding under the table especially delicious.

World War II: The Early War Years

The Germans took over Austria in 1938 and marched into Czechoslovakia in 1939. They had already been allowed, by concession of the British and French, to annex the Sudetenland, that region of Czechoslovakia along the German border which was inhabited almost exclusively by German-speaking people.

Hitler's propaganda machine had very successfully agitated the rest of the German minority in Czechoslovakia. He promised the end to preference in bank loans to Czech farmers and businesses, he fabricated grievances and incidents to provoke Germans to violence against Czechs and on March 15, 1939, under the pretext of offering "protection to the German population against bodily harm from the Czech majority," Hitler's armies marched into the heart of Czechoslovakia. The rest of the world, although stunned, did nothing.

I was 13 years old.

It was a stormy March day. Dirty, half-melted snow covered the huge "Marktplatz" the town square in Iglau. Parked along the snow banks on the edges of the square were German tanks and large lorries. Other military vehicles covered, or so it seemed, the entire cobblestoned square. Soldiers were everywhere and we children from the German gymnasium were allowed to ladle out hot soup from portable canteens. Later on that afternoon, all of the students from my school lined up to wait for Herr Hitler in person.

He was supposed to arrive at any minute and excitement made us forget the penetrating cold. Iglau (now Jihlava) and the surrounding villages were a mostly German speaking enclave called a "Sprachinsel"—an ethnic German island. This is why the German army had stopped en masse here—it was friendly territory.

It was night when Hitler finally arrived, but I still remember him standing on the podium, looking just as we know him from old TV reels—stiff, arm raised in salute, in boots and Nazi uniform. I remember his slightly bulging eyes, the small moustache, and the raspy voice as he spoke about freeing the German population of the hated yoke of Czech domination. I did not know anything about hate or the value of hate for propaganda reasons. I just thought him mesmerizing and I told my parents so.

My parents did not contradict me at the time. They were already aware that a negative remark, carelessly repeated, could prove disastrous for my family.

Some of the German officers of the tank division were billeted in our house. These officers were not Nazis, they were gentlemen who had chosen the army as a career as had their fathers before them and who would soon be confronted with the moral dilemma of having a lunatic murderer as Commander in Chief. Some of them were killed in the war; some later on became involved in the effort to have Hitler assassinated and were hanged in reprisal. None of those officers survived the war.

Within a few months, the Germans had taken over every aspect of government. It was the beginning of years of fear, of deprivation and personal hardship and the holocaust of war and persecution.

I learned that my great-grandfather and grandfather, although baptized, were Jews, my mother was half-Jewish and my sisters and I were one-quarter Jewish. The laws of Nuremburg, by which the Germans decreed who was ethnically "pure" and who was not, applied to my family.

Still, I was required to participate in all activities of the Hitler Youth, but was denied the "Tuch und Knoten," the scarf and leather ring which completed the uniform of blue skirt and white shirt. This was, of course, terribly humiliating as I had been the star athlete of my class at school. As a World War I hero, my father declined the honor of joining the German army, which did not endear him to the new regime. One of my great aunts who was married to a Jewish gentleman disappeared into the concentration camp "Theresienstadt" and perished there. Friends around us were arrested for speaking out against Hitler's regime, or for trumped-up treason charges which were fabricated in order to get hold of their estates or business.

On the first of September 1939, Hitler rolled into Poland and World War II was upon us.

My cousin Peter Seidl was serving as a 1st Lt. on the Polish front when he learned that his uncle and grandmother, his only relatives after his parents had perished years earlier in a car accident, had died in a double suicide in Iglau.

Tante Emma, my grandfather Theodor's sister, the same great aunt with whom we stayed during our school years in Iglau, had been denounced by her maid for listening to the BBC Radio, something the population was forbidden to do. She was over eighty years old but arrest would surely follow. The fact that although married to a gentile, she was Jewish by birth, would weigh heavily against her. Her son, a lawyer in Prague, came to Iglau and shot his mother and then himself.

Peter was given leave to come to the funeral and stayed with us. He made a will, leaving everything to my older sister Marietta, who had been his closest childhood companion. He told us, before he went back to the Eastern front, that he did not intend to fight for a Germany he had come to despise. He was killed two weeks later. In bitter irony, he was awarded a high medal posthumously. The double suicide and wanton death of my cousin affected all of us deeply.

Life went on, but we learned to speak carefully to the world at large—seething inwardly at the cruelties committed around us, disappointed in former friends who embraced the Nazi doctrine and sorrowful at the constant news of death from the war front of people who died not for the love of country, but because they were caught up in a war they could not escape.

Some, even in my own family, took measures that made life easier for them.

Two of my mother's siblings, my aunt Hetty and my uncle Hans, had themselves "aryanized". They persuaded my poor grandmother to swear to the authorities that they had been conceived out of wedlock and therefore could not be "Jewish." For their father, she had to name an old friend of the family, by then long deceased. Both Hetty and Hans looked like my grandmother, with blue eyes and upturned nose, and that seemed to be sufficient physical evidence to declare them "ethnically pure." My grandmother, although she adored Hetty and especially Hans, must have suffered greatly by the indignity inflicted upon her and the shamefulness of the lie. Needless to say, our relationship with both these relatives became strained from then on.

My older sister Marietta, who had been in boarding school in Switzerland in 1939, came back and was immediately targeted for the "Arbeitsdienst"—"arbeit" meaning "work" and "dienst" meaning "duty"—to work on a farm in the absence of the male farmers. Such work was often backbreaking and could prove ruinous to the health of women not used to such hard labor.

To avoid random assignment, parents tried to place their daughters with friends who had large farms and were eligible for help. But first, my sister had her perfectly healthy appendix removed. Time out for convalescence meant this gained valuable time for her. She eventually "served" on a large estate in northern Germany belonging to friends.

After finishing the cooking school in Iglau, I also had to enter the work force. At the age of 17 I was assigned as a maid to a good Nazi family in Vienna. It was called the "Duty Year" for younger girls. Again, through some contacts, I was assigned to a family known to my parents. There was only one child, but the grandmother was a Nazi high up in the hierarchy who proudly wore the "golden swastika" on her lapel. Her daughter was the mother of the child I cared for. I also had to cook and clean.

But my employer was a member of Vienna society, and as a social equal, she treated me more as a friend than a maid, and her ghastly mother did not visit often. Her husband, again through his mother-in-law's pull, although in the Army, was stationed in Northern Italy. He would come home frequently, always laden with food no longer available in Vienna. I stayed with them for almost a year during which time some fierce bombings of Vienna occurred.

I don't remember if I was in Vienna when St. Stephen's Cathedral and the Opera House were bombed, but I do remember the daily attacks. Some came in the morning, some at night.

The high alarm whistle would go off and we would gather a few belongings and the baby and make for the air-raid shelter. You came to know most of the people who shared the shelter. I remember one gentleman who owned farms in Slovakia and who was always well equipped with salami, good bread and especially an inexhaustible supply of good cognac, which he shared generously. The cognac helped, because the attacks were frightening. First came the deep hum of the approaching heavy bomber aircraft. Then, the anti-aircraft guns started firing. After that we waited for the high whistle of the falling bombs and the detonations on impact. If they were close, you took another swig of the cognac.

When it was all over you came out, not knowing if your house still stood, saying a silent prayer of thanks if it did.

I once went up to the roof of my building during an attack. The night sky was lit up by search lights—the sound of the anti-aircraft guns was deafening and I could see the American bombers overhead. While I watched, one was hit and burst into flames. I saw parachutes in the sky and saw them being shot down by anti-aircraft. It was a very sobering experience. I dreamed for a long time about the airmen whose parachutes had opened only to be shot at by the Germans.

By the fall of 1944, the family I worked for announced they would leave Vienna. The Nazi grandmother decided that the safest place would be western Austria, close to the Swiss border. I did not want to go with them; I wanted to go home and asked them to have me transferred for War Duty to my grandfather's former factory. That factory had been confiscated from the owners and had become a factory producing parts for fighter airplanes.

I was lucky. Without further ado, the family not only let me go, they managed to have me transferred to Altenberg.

I went home, and in the fall of 1944 started working at the factory which, as you may remember, was only minutes away from our house.

Work in the Factory: 1944

I was glad to be home in peaceful Czechoslovakia after the fearful time of living in Vienna during the bombardment.

My parents were well and my younger sister was still in school in Iglau. Marietta, my older sister, was in Vienna working for a German censorship agency, censoring the mail of French workers who were forced to work in Germany and lived in camps.

Marietta had studied French and taken the interpreter's exam after doing her "Arbeitsdienst".

After completion of her studies, she had been assigned to this censorship agency in Vienna. Slowly she had established a connection with the French Underground and her apartment in Vienna had become one of the way-stations for escaped laborers on their way back to France. This was highly dangerous work, all of course unknown to my parents in Altenberg.

Marietta stayed until the very last moment in Vienna. But finally, with the Russians at the gates of Vienna, she came home to Altenberg early in 1945.

The factory I was assigned to employed about 3,000 workers, many of whom were political prisoners, or like me, worked there as part of "War Duty."

Pay was minimal; working hours were from 6 a.m. to 6 p.m. and every week you shifted from day to night duty, 6 p.m. to 6 a.m. Looking back now, I marvel how I adjusted to the constant shift from day to night work. But I felt lucky. I could sleep at home and supplement my diet with food at home.

I worked in that factory from September 1944 to March 1945. I was assigned to kitchen duty and peeled potatoes for hours every day.

Sometimes we received a shipment of rabbits which had to be skinned, before cooking. We made endless dumplings and watery soup.

We often had to leave everything to rush into air raid shelters. Allied bombers flew overhead to bomb larger targets near Prague—but you never knew. I remember coming back from the air-raid trenches to find that the dough we had been mixing with yeast for the daily dumplings, had worked its way off the tables onto the rather dirty floor. We just scooped up the dough and produced "marbled" dumplings. Sanitary conditions certainly were not good in that vast makeshift kitchen—but I do not remember anyone getting sick during all the months I was there.

It was during my time at the factory that I became involved in some underground work. Dispensing food daily at various "windows" to the workers, we also fed the political prisoners who worked there, always under heavy guard. I would be given messages on thin paper, which, tightly rolled, I inserted into a dumpling and served to a particular prisoner who seemed to be the leader. My heart would pound as I tried to carefully ladle that particular dumpling onto the right plate. I was always afraid I would somehow miss the designated plate and thus miss the right prisoner. Some of my friends did more dangerous deeds. They would insert wooden pins instead of steel pins into delicate parts of the motors they were building. These faulty parts would withstand the trial runs of the completed motors before shipment. How long it was before they failed I do not know.

By March of 1945, the end seemed near. The German engineers, guards and other personnel were disappearing from one day to the next, and finally, we were released from the factory—at least I was—and somber consideration was given to "what to do when the end came."

Family Anecdotes and History

My younger sister Christine was a very quiet and shy child. She played endlessly with her dolls and doll-house, talking in a slow murmur for hours, quite oblivious of the goings-on around her. When she was about ten or eleven, she began to sleepwalk; in her case she would take a pitcher and "water her flowers" by emptying it over my head. I would awake, wet and outraged, and run into my parents' bedroom to report the awful deed. My parents sympathized, talked to Christine, and even consulted our family doctor. I can't quite remember how they broke my sister of the habit, but for a time I was moved to another room.

My cousin Nikki and I, at the age of about twelve or thirteen, found the learned bible on "Sex in Marriage" behind the works of Schiller in the library. We would pour over this extremely dry and unintelligible tome of medical phraseology in the hope for enlightenment. Frustrated, we finally sent away for a copy of something more modern and spent the rest of the summer hiding high in a tree being "enlightened."

We certainly were not given the facts of life by our parents. Our mother tried the "birds and bees" method, but although we saw animals coupling and puppies being born, we never connected animals to people. We learned more in due course from the village children, but even at seventeen and eighteen, we were only told by our parents that a "Cavallar" did not do this or that, and a "Cavallar" always behaved like a lady. Whatever that was, we only knew vaguely

My parents had a box at the Opera in Iglau. We children were encouraged to attend and be educated and although the performances were somewhat second-rate, they were often amusing.

I remember a performance of "Tosca" where Tosca, once she realizes that her lover has indeed been shot dead, throws herself off the parapet of Castle Sant'Angelo. She obviously jumped onto a springy mattress below, only to be catapulted halfway up so that with the dying note of her aria she reappeared on stage. It was hilarious and we immediately incorporated "Tosca's last moments" into our annual plays. Naturally, we also learned to sing her aria....

My grandmother Heda, known as "Maemchen," lived with us in Altenberg. She was born in Cologne, Germany into a military family. When she married my grandfather Theoodor Kern, she married into great wealth, quite unlike her well-born, but not wealthy background.

She must have been a very pretty girl, with a lovely profile, good figure and very good legs. My grandfather Theodor was 14 years older than she.

Maemchen was vain, concerned with self, but jolly.

She constantly massaged and creamed herself and always arranged her skirts so that her legs and pretty feet could be admired. In her seventies, she became quite deaf but refused to wear a hearing aid.

Her mind became fixated on death and sex. If someone mentioned the lovely weather, she would loudly ask "who died???" If one of us packed an overnight case to spend the night with friends, she would admonish our mother with: "How can you allow her to go off unchaperoned, especially since I saw her pack her hair curlers? I don't like to THINK what she might be up to!" Of course we took advantage of her mind set and would tell her outrageous stories. She took it, however, all in good grace.

She loved to be the center of any event, and later on, during the war, when we had parties downstairs to which we did not invite her, she would retaliate by sending her maid, Maria Kuplien, downstairs to retrieve a silver tray with small liqueur glasses, used to offer after-dinner drinks. The tray was hers and Maria had to say "her Grace needs it upstairs." My father always warned the guests to "drink up quickly, as their glasses might disappear at any moment."

During the war, when skirts became quite short again, my grandmother decided to shorten her skirts as well. She bent down in front of a mirror and equipped with large scissors cut her hem to the desired length. When she straightened up however, the hem was halfway up her thigh.

If we traveled anywhere and something did not go according to plan, she always told us: "If I had known that, I would have stayed at home." It became a much quoted saying in times of adversity in our family.

Maemchen did not want to use the "Heil Hitler" greeting, although we were required to. On her walks she would raise her walking stick and cheerfully shout "Hi He" "Hi He," which she assumed would suffice.

She came with us when we fled to Austria. She sat on her down quilt in the car, covered herself with it when we cowered in ditches during fighter plane attacks and behaved like a trooper all through the journey.

Her oldest daughter, Tante Detta, had been evacuated to Bavaria in the last days of the war and once we arrived in Austria, my grandmother wanted to join her. Marietta and I put her on a train in Salzburg. The train was bombed and the survivors were returned to Salzburg and housed on straw pallets in a half-bombed hotel near the railroad station. Two weeks after she had left, we were contacted by the Red Cross and asked to pick her up.

She was in terrible shape, emaciated, unwashed, and what was worse, quite out of her mind. She recovered somewhat but we were happy when, after the end of the war, we were able to locate uncle Hans in Vienna and turn her over to him. She lived into her eighties but never fully recovered her senses.

Tante Detta (Margarethe), my mother's oldest sister, survived the war in Bavaria. She had been the "bluestocking" in the family. She lived for years in Berlin with her old English governess and ran a book shop. In Bavaria she met a widower and the two married and became the happiest of couples. They returned to Berlin and lived contented for many years.

Tante Hetty, who became an "Aryan" during the war and whose husband had been one of the executives in Mr. Ribbentrop's champagne business, came to live as a refugee in Upper Austria. Their son Nikki, who had been my childhood companion, survived the war but died young.

Onkel Hans became a well-known comedian on the stage in Vienna after the war. He married and had two daughters.

My father was one of 10 children—six boys and four girls. Only one, Uncle Hans, embraced the Third Reich. Ferdinand, the first born, had been an officer in the fledgling Austrian Air Force during World War I, and continued his involvement with the air industry between the wars. Walther married well and produced one daughter, Eva, who with her husband, Helge Forster, now lives in Kitzbühel, Austria and Lucerne, Switzerland. Max did very well in Vienna as an engineer. He had one daughter who married Tono von Reininghaus and now lives in Kitzbühel. Kurt died early. Of the girls, Gretl married and had one son, Walther Kiss, who is married and lives in Kitzbühel. Lene never married; neither did Mimi. Emmy, quite late in life, married Baron Camillo Buschmann, who was a lawyer in Kitzbühel.

They had no children and became my surrogate parents while I lived in Salzburg and taught me how to ski. I spent many, many happy times in their house and loved both of them dearly.

Of our faithful employees, Euli, as already mentioned, married the local blacksmith and died in her nineties, just a few years ago. Rosi and Anton stayed with my parents through the Russian occupation. Maria Kuplien returned to Yugoslavia where she had originally come from. She visited my parents in Vienna a few times after they came out of Altenberg. She also wrote long and wonderful letters which always started: "With deep humility, wonderful Frau Baronin (my mother), I joyfully reach for my pen to express my respect and devotion."

She remained a faithful friend of the family until she died.

My Aunt Rosa

My aunt Rosa was not a blood relative; she was my very eccentric godmother. My christening present from her was a bowl, hollow at the bottom, that, when filled with hot water, kept food warm for the eating child. These plates were popular in my childhood and usually had a pretty picture on the enamel surface of the bowl—you had to eat yourself through to the picture. My bowl, however, was of solid silver, quite heavy and, since it tarnished and had to be polished constantly, was never used.

Some years later, "Tante Rosl" as I called her, asked my mother to let her have the bowl back so that she could use it for another christening. I felt I had been robbed—and told her so. She understood and during the war years she tried to make up for "my loss" with frequent gifts.

One I remember vividly: a pair of clip-on earrings made of glass beads in the form of grape clusters. They were quite beautiful but heavy and pinched my ears dreadfully. When my ear lobes turned black and blue, I was forbidden to wear them. I, however, would have continued to suffer, just to be "beautiful."

Tante Rosa was a strikingly beautiful woman, very tall, very elegant, with jet-black hair and large dark eyes. At a time when using too much rouge, too much perfume or painting one's fingernails was not considered ladylike, she seemed to flaunt all conventions. Women of my parents' social circle, although fascinated by her, professed to detest her. My father thought that she was not quite a lady, but always became quite animated in her presence. My mother found her amusing, wise in the ways of the world and quite adored her.

Tante Rosa was addicted to smuggling forbidden items across borders. I remember waiting with my father at our local train station for her to return from a trip to Hungary. During the war, Hungary had food items that were no longer available to us. True to form, she had fastened an entire salami under her skirts around her waist. As she descended the steep steps of the train, the salami under her skirt rose like a phallic symbol with each step she took. People sniggered, my father blanched in embarrassment and I shook with suppressed laughter.

At the end of World War II, she turned her house in the south of France into a recuperation center for wounded U.S. soldiers. As a reward, she somehow managed to get a visa to visit Czechoslovakia in 1946, dressed as a Red Cross official. She visited all her friends, including my parents, and offered to take anyone's jewelry out of Czechoslovakia to safely deposit it in a bank in the American Zone of Occupation. We all knew that it was only a matter of time before all landowners with large estates would have to abandon their homes and become refugees in the western part of Europe.

Into a leather pouch, therefore, went diamond rings, brooches and pearl necklaces. She made no list as to what belonged to whom—they were all friends and would reclaim only what belonged to them. Well, eventually somebody slipped up and took a brooch that belonged to someone else, and my aunt Rosa was in BIG trouble. She was accused of stealing and went to jail for a short time. Luckily, the missing diamond brooch turned up and everyone was happy and appropriately grateful.

My godmother lived to be about ninety years old. No longer wealthy, she nevertheless never lost her sense of adventure and joy of life. She even managed to acquire a title late in life by briefly marrying a misbehaving offspring of a well known family. She offered her house on the Rivera for the young man to disappear to in exchange for his name. To be addressed as "countess" appealed to her, especially in beauty salons, where she liked to be bowed to, and at restaurants where she claimed to get superior service.

I always visit her grave when I am in Vienna—I leave a red rose, her favorite flower.

The Flight to Austria

I started a diary in March of 1945. Rereading it, I can sense the anxiety on every page. There was the knowledge that the world as we knew it was about to crumble around us and that decisions would have to be made that led, at best, into an unknown future.

Friends, or friends of friends, began to arrive, begging for a bed for a night, only to disappear to God knows where the next day. These people were full of news from the war front, about the unraveling of the Third Reich, about the approaching Russian Army and the pillage, rape and murder that followed in their wake. "Leave", they all said, "Leave, while you still can."

Listening to the radio for news, you were treated to the music of "Le Prelude" by Franz List, music designated by the Germans to precede news from the Eastern Front—always positive. Although the Russians had penetrated deep into German territory, we were told how "the heroic German Army was driving the enemy back …"—news that everyone knew were pathetic fabrications. If you dared, you turned to the news of the BBC out of London—THEIR signature tune was the first bars of Beethoven's Fifth Symphony. One no longer played the Fifth for the sake of music. If it was overheard, you might be accused of listening to forbidden broadcasts—an act of treason.

Erwein Honsig, a neighbor of ours, decided to send his wife and children to a farm he owned near Salzburg. My younger sister was taken out of school and accompanied them to Austria. He planned to follow them later, leaving his large estate in the hands of some trusted employees. He had hidden a car, although by 1944, all of us had to turn private cars over to the authorities to be used for the war effort. Honsig now made this car ready to leave at a moment's notice.

The leader of the local Communist Party came to see my father and told him that he and his followers were willing to protect my parents. This was important: we were, after all, the largest house around and were of Austrian descent, speaking German not Czech. My parents were beloved in the entire neighborhood, not only as landlords, but as anti-Nazis; would that be enough?

The Communist leader assured them that, following some basic rules, they would be able to shield them. However, they insisted that none of us girls could remain. They would hide their own daughters from the first wave of Russian soldiers, but they could not guarantee our safety.

The decision was made that my older sister Marietta and I would leave with Erwein Honsig whenever he was ready. At the last moment, my grandmother was added to the party.

With four people in the car, there was only minimum space for luggage. The boot of the car was filled with barter items, mostly meat, some potatoes, some blankets which could be used if we had to spend a night in the car, and extra petrol. My grandmother had her down comforter on which she sat elevated, like a queen.

We left at 3 a.m. on a cold April morning and I remember craning my neck to get a last glimpse of my parents standing forlornly in the dawn light, waving to us.

The Russians occupied our village 12 days later. My parents survived, although they had more than 100 Russians quartered on straw pellets in the house. Luckily, they also had some of the Russian officers billeted in the house who would keep the soldiers in check.

While my father was dealing with the Russians "upstairs," my mother tended to the frightened women of the village who were hiding in cellars under the house. Many had been raped repeatedly—all were scared to death—but my mother very courageously fed them, tended to their medical needs and even delivered a baby down there by candlelight.

My mother, although barely fifty-years-old at the time, made herself unattractive with loose clothing and babushka like scarves to escape the attention of the soldiers. She was also lucky: one of the soldiers saw her as a mother figure and slept in front of my parents' bedroom door to "protect" her. I know that the soldiers threatened to execute my father several times, but in the end, they were not harmed. When the soldiers left, they stole all the bicycles, which they wrapped in oriental rugs to hide their theft, but they took little else. My parents were extremely fortunate. Other people did not fare as well.

But back to our journey to Austria.

We had very little gasoline for the long trip and hoped to refuel along the way in some manner or other.

On the first day, in late afternoon, it was strangely enough a staff car full of SS officers who gave us some gasoline when we had almost run out and were trying to stop cars asking for help.

My grandmother in the back of the car was scared witless by their uniforms swarming around the car. Being very hard of hearing she thought they were going to arrest us. My sister and I had to tell her in no uncertain terms to be q u i e t!

Full up with gas we proceeded driving south. It was slow going as the road was congested with refugees in cars, horse-drawn wagons, on bicycles and on foot going south away from the advancing Russians, and on the other side of the road, the German army was moving north toward the enemy.

Once in a while, American fighter planes would swoop down out of the sky to attack the column of German army trucks. Everyone of course dove for shelter, under cars and into the ditches along the road, hoping for the best. We were lucky; further on along the road we saw burned-out vehicles and the dead and the wounded.

Some of the pork in the back of the car secured us shelter for the first night on the edge of the Boemerwald, the mountainous forest that is the natural southern border of Czechoslovakia. Continuing the next morning, we were again low on gas and as we drove through the dense forest we came upon a German truck, parked and unattended at the edge of the road. Lo and behold, the open truck was filled with gasoline cans, whether empty or full we did not know. At any rate, my beautiful older sister was sent into the forest to find and to delay the occupants, while Erwein Honsig and I scrambled onto the truck and grabbed two full canisters of petrol. Safely back in the car, we waited for my sister to emerge from the woods, laughing and chatting with several soldiers—and once she was back in the car, we quickly drove off.

By late afternoon of that day we came to a military check-point at the Inn River and were told we could not cross, as the bridge was about to be blown up. Frantic, we begged to be allowed to cross and finally traded the rest of the meat and potatoes in the back of the car for that privilege.

Safely across and now on Austrian soil, we proceeded toward what we hoped would be shelter for the coming night—the chateau of friends, the Count Arco, in St. Martin in Upper Austria. Arriving at the gates of the imposing chateau, we were again stopped by military sentry and told that the chateau was filled with refugees and also with the horses of the Spanish Riding School, their riders and grooms.

My sister Marietta knew Col. Podhaisky, the head of the Spanish Riding School from her days in Vienna, and the combination of knowing the owners as well as the head of the Riding School gained us admittance.

We spent the night—my grandmother and I on sofas in the Grand Ballroom, my older sister in the private apartments of the Countess. Erwein Honsig slept in the car, afraid that with all those refugees around, it might disappear. That night we did listen to the BBC beaming news into Europe and learned that the Americas were pushing fast into Austria from the West. Dachau, the infamous concentration camp, had been liberated. That brought out some hidden champagne as Josi Arco's husband had been a prisoner in Dachau. We all drank to his survival and a safe return.

He did survive the camp, but tragically lost his life on the way home, when the jeep he was riding in overturned and killed him and the driver.

The next morning, after watching the Lipizzaner horses being exercised, we continued on our journey and arrived a few hours later in the village of Henndorf, our destination. As irony will have it, the car that had so valiantly carried us all this way gave up its ghost at the bottom of a long hill, in sight of the farm house which would be our home for the coming months. We had to be fetched by horse and buggy.

When told that the Lipizzaner horses had escaped Vienna and were in St. Martin, General Patton, the famous American Army commander, visited the chateau of Count Arco. And when he was told that the mares were still in Czechoslovakia, in a daring move Patton sent U.S. soldiers into Bohemia to round up the mares and drive them into the part of Austria occupied by American forces.

He thus saved the breed and became an instant hero in Austria. Although the Russians very much wanted the Americans to give up the horses of the Spanish Riding School, that never came to pass, thanks to General Patton.

Last Days of the War and the Summer of 1945

Henndorf is a village about 20 kilometers east of Salzburg located on the Wallersee, one of the many lakes of that region. It is an idyllic spot and the farm of our friends was meant to be a self-supporting vacation spot. Beautifully furnished with antiques and big enough with several bedrooms, it was still a typical farm in the style of the Salzburg foothills, stables and barn attached to the main house, stone foundation and upper story of wood with a balcony along the front facade.

In the last days of the war, it became the refuge of Erwein's entire family—his wife, his two children, his mother-in-law, the family cook and now the three Cavallar sisters. In addition, there was the caretaker couple and one male worker from Czechoslovakia.

Within days of our arrival, the caretaker couple and the farm hand decided to go back to Altenberg. They took a wagon and two horses and, as we learned later, did make it back home.

In the meantime Erwein was left with a houseful of women to try to run the farm. There were about 15 cows, chickens, several horses and meadows surrounding the farm that would have to be mowed and the hay brought under cover for winter feeding.

The cows were still milked by hand. Christine, my sixteen-year-old sister, was designated to learn how to milk. Along with Erwein she milked the cows.

I was assigned to the kitchen to help the ancient cook who was no longer capable of dealing creatively with meager supplies and feed so many people.

Alix, our hostess was to take care of the chickens, feed them, collect the eggs and keep the chicken coop clean. Alix hated chickens and hated her job, but valiantly did the best she could. She gave the chickens names and one could hear her in the morning calling: "Rosamunde, Akeleia, Orphelia, you miserable beasts, do your duty and lay eggs!!"

Marietta, my older sister who loved to ride, was put in charge of the horses, and every day she rode about the countryside reconnoitering. She gathered information about the advancing American Army, German military resistance and where additional food supplies could be bought.

There were days when she came back to announce that in some house in the village, German soldiers were giving away cigarettes, in packets of 100, or sugar, or what went for coffee in those last days of the war. The soldiers were bartering all these items for civilian clothes so that they could blend into the population when the end came.

We would rush to the scene, with whatever containers we could handle, and barter or buy. The cigarettes were dry and tasted like straw, but we all started smoking and when we could no longer hold on to the stumps, would empty the residue onto a plate and roll our own cigarettes. Bad for the lungs, but since these cigarettes tasted so badly and burned your lungs if you inhaled, I never did learn to inhale, even later on when "good" cigarettes were available.

I remember the day when we came upon a cache of brown sugar. We bought several large bags and I would produce a milk-soup for dinner, consisting of milk thickened with flour and topped with brown sugar. I am sure it was pretty awful, but deprived as we were of sugar, it tasted heavenly.

I learned how to bake bread from the farmer's wife down the hill. In a large wooden trough I poured about 40 kg of flour—a mixture of rye and wheat—liberally sprinkled salt and caraway seeds onto the flour, and added yeast mixed with warm water. Now the real mixing started. I added more warm water till all the flour had become a dough that I could further mix by using both my hands and arms up to my armpits. When I had achieved the right consistency, I would hack off some dough with a wooden spatula and on a wooden board liberally sprinkled with flour, I would knead the dough with my right hand against my left, till I had formed a round loaf that was smooth and without wrinkles.

The latter was terribly important: if the loaves retained wrinkles, they would eventually burst while baking and create an uneven loaf. Each loaf was then put into a straw basket and with all windows closed (to avoid any drafts) was left to rise overnight.

The baking took place in an outdoor oven, shaped like an igloo. The inside of the oven was made of round river stones. Wood was burned in the oven till the stones were very hot. The ashes were removed and the oven would then be ready for my baking.

I would put each loaf (nicely risen overnight) on a long shovel-like stick and deposit the loaf onto the hot stones. The trick was to sort of flip the loaf off the handle before it started to expand and be dragged out by the handle. I ruined many a loaf before I learned "the flip".

After one hour of baking, each loaf was taken out, rubbed with cold water (to create a shiny crust) and put back to bake for a bit longer, I have forgotten how long.

I made 20 loaves of bread every two weeks.

By the end of April 1945, everyone was just waiting for the end. There no longer was a functioning government. Shelves in the stores were bare and only people like us, who lived on farms, had enough to eat.

One had to be very vigilant, as strangers appeared from nowhere, asking for food or threatening us if we could not give them what they asked for. Luckily we spoke English, French, Italian, Czech and some Russian between us and were able to communicate with these strangers. They were deserters, prisoners of war, forced labor workers, displaced persons—people from all over Europe trying to walk home, wherever that was.

We would give everybody something to eat and then hope they would leave peacefully. We were lucky, perhaps because we spoke their languages; some of the other farms did not fare as well. German officers came with their horses, begging us to take their beautiful animals as they needed rest and grazing and they feared they would have to shoot them. My sister Marietta could never say no to their pleas and soon we had more horses than was really acceptable. We lost one cow to an American fighter plane which was obviously shooting at the retreating German Army on the main road. The cow was quickly turned into barter meat and some of the meat was pickled and used in our cooking.

On May 7th, the unconditional surrender of the Armies of the Third Reich was announced.

That evening we all marched down the hill to the main road to watch the Americans drive by in their jeeps. We cheered and welcomed them in English, but they never looked left or right.

Within days we met our first American soldiers. They drove up in jeeps and lorries looking for fresh butter and eggs. They offered chocolate, chewing gum (a new experience for us), K-rations and soap as barter. All these items were most welcome and we were happy to do the exchange.

Word got around in the village that we spoke English and soon we had more visitors than we could handle. Marietta and I found employment in the village as interpreters. Henndorf was occupied by a company of black soldiers with white officers. We had never seen black people before, and the village children howled with fear when they encountered them. However, the soldiers made friends in the village very quickly. They were kind and very generous in sharing with the population things that were available to them, such as food and cigarettes.

Toward the end of their stay, they threw a big party for the entire village—they had food and sweets and cigarettes and chewing gum for the children and whisky and local schnapps and wine.

Nine months later, some very dark babies were baptized in the local church by our kind village priest. We invited some of the officers to the farm for a rather formal dinner presided over by Alix Honsig's mother, a rather formidable lady of the old school. The officers came in full uniform and were on their best behavior, pulling out chairs for the ladies and making polite conversation.

Afterwards, Alix' mother commented a bit waspishly: "These men were very polite, but had no table manners. They cut their meat and put their knife down to switch the fork to their right hand and to make matters worse, their left hand, when not used for eating, always rested under the table." We had absolutely no idea that these were perfect table manners in the U.S.A!

Spring had turned into early summer and the grass was high enough to be cut. Erwein spent hours cutting the meadows with a grass cutter pulled by two horses and at the edge of the meadows he would use a scythe, rhythmically swinging it to and fro. This was backbreaking work—but equally backbreaking was our work, slowly turning the grass with rakes by hand, row after row, hour after hour.

The summer of 1945 was sunny and hot and after the grass had turned into hay, we had to rake piles which were then lifted up to a hay wagon pulled by two horses. Marietta always held the horses, an easy job, whereas the rest of us raked and raked and lifted and stuffed the hay onto the wagon.

Once we had brought the wagon into the barn, we had to lift the hay with pitch forks up into the loft. I have never worked that hard before or since, but my memory is full of laughter at our inadequacy.

How poor Erwein put up with us, I don't know. Once, on a particularly hot day we were turning the hay down by a stream when Erwein appeared on the horizon telling us to work faster. Without a word, we all shed our clothes and jumped into the cold stream. Erwein retreated out of modesty.

We had of course no news of our parents, just as they did not know how we were. It was not until August of 1945 that a friend stopped by the farm with news that our parents had survived the Russian occupation. This person was going back to Czechoslovakia and took letters from us with him.

Fall and Winter 1945

All through the summer of 1945, visiting friends had told us about the possibilities of employment with the U.S. Occupation Forces in Salzburg. In August, my sister Marietta departed for Salzburg where she had found a job with the liaison officer for the French Occupation Forces in Austria. She later on moved to Innsbruck, which was in the French zone of occupation. As recognition for her undercover work in helping French forced labor workers to escape during the war, she was awarded honorary French citizenship and in later years worked at the French Embassy in Vienna.

It was time for me to go to work as well and to arrange for Christine to finish her education at the Gymnasium in Salzburg.

After a few interviews with several departments of the administration departments of the Occupation Forces, I was sent to the headquarters of Counter Intelligence whose agents needed "indigenous" personnel to do translation work.

I was hired on the spot, although the officer who hired me told me later that I presented quite an amusing sight. Hiking boots over white socks, a somewhat worn homespun skirt and white blouse, hair cut short by my sister and obviously without style, sunburned nose and work-worn, blistered hands and an inordinate amount of lipstick, courtesy of a friend at my previous interview. As the pièce de résistance, this friend had stuck a flower into my hair for further beautification.

We had left Czechoslovakia with very few clothes and there had been little opportunity in the months after the war to replenish our wardrobes. Cosmetics were quite unknown to me, as even at home we girls had not used any. I do not remember how soon I was able to acquire more to wear, but since everyone was in a similar situation it did not seem to matter.

I did ruin my feet, however. Shoes just were impossible to buy—one "inherited" shoes from someone who more often than not had a different shoe size.

Since the weather remained warm and dry, I rode my bicycle every day to work in Salzburg. Going into town was not too bad, as it was mostly downhill, but coming home after work was a long and hard journey. On most hills I had to push the bike as I also had to do on the last part up to the farm. It probably took me 2 ½ hours each day to come home. Sometimes I hitched a ride on an Army truck, but it soon became evident that I could not continue to live in Henndorf.

Erwein's mother and sisters lived in a lovely old villa in a suburb of Salzburg and they kindly offered me a former servant's room under the eves of the house and to share their food with me. My job gave me a full Army ration-type meal at lunch. I did not need much at night.

My poor sister Christine, on the other hand, had to walk every day to catch the local train (which in the winter became a true hardship) and from the train station to her school which started at 8 a. m. After school she took the train home again where she still helped to milk cows in addition to doing her homework.

After a long and beautiful summer, the winter of 1945 was very severe with extremely cold temperatures and heavy snowfall. There was still not enough food and very little wood or coal to heat houses or apartments. People suffered but made do as best they could.

My room at the villa had become so cold that water in pots put onto the floor to catch rain from the leaky roof had frozen solid. One day, one of my American bosses took me home in his jeep and demanded to see my room. He was horrified and the following day took me around town to look for another place for me to live.

We found a room with a wonderful elderly couple who were happy to rent me their "salon" and promised to heat the tall, tiled stove daily.

They treated me like a daughter, eventually met my parents and for six years provided me with a loving and stable home.

My room, furnished as a salon in the Empire style, consisted mostly of uncomfortable period chairs and my bed was an Empire-style sofa. The mattress that had been put on the sofa to make it more comfortable tilted somewhat toward the floor so that one had to be careful not to slide off. But I had a soft pillow, warm blankets and a lamp so that I could read in bed. I felt extremely happy to have found such comfort.

My sister Christine, during exams, would spend the night with me, sleeping on a makeshift bed on the floor, which was better than the awful trek back to Henndorf. I used the kitchen to prepare my meals and like any good daughter, I would present my dates to Frau Generalin before I went out.

In 1965, when I came to Austria with my son Christopher, I introduced him to Frau Generalin. She was a widow by then, as her husband, who had been a general in World War I, had died some years earlier.

Factory stationery with villa on right, circa 1900

My grandmother (Maemchen)

My grandfather Theodor

My mother

My father

My father with his medals. The Maria Theresia Cross is the simple white enamel cross on his right side of his tunic.

Emperor Karl of Austria awarding the Maria Theresia Cross to my father

Empress Zita of Austria addressing my father.

Villa "Altenberg"

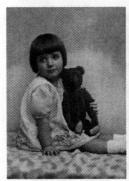

Dorli with teddybear

Marietta, Dorli and Christl, circa 1931

On the summit of Kitzsteinhorn,
2,900 meters, circa 1950

Dorli racing in "May Race"
Arthurhaus, 1949

Dorli giving a snack to a racer, 1949

View of Kitzsteinhorn

The farm in Henndorf

The three sisters, the summer of 1945

Working hard to bring in the hay

Immigration on the USNS
"General Sturgis," April, 1951

View of the Manhattan
skyline from the ship

IRO
International Movements Office
Bagagge Department - Camp Grohn

BAGGAGE CHECK № 525

Ship: **USNS "General Sturgis"**
From: **Bremerhaven** to: **New York (USA)**
Date of Sailing: **11ᵗʰ April 1951**
For Passenger Number: ....

Baggage tag from sailing, April 11, 1951

Wedding to Thomas Charles Mason, 1953

Our house in Madison, Connecticut

Christopher's christening, with grandmother
Cavallar on my right and grandmother Mason on my left.

Henndorf 1965

Christopher growing up in Madison

Hiking and skiing with Chris in the Mount Rainier region, 1997

Christmas, 1986

Skiing in St. Anton am Arlberg, 1981

Working for CIC: 1945–47

I started my job at the offices of CIC (Counter Intelligence Corps) in Salzburg on Sept. 15, 1945.

I was put in charge of the switchboard, taking incoming calls, connecting calls to the various offices and doing typing. I did not know how to type and I certainly did not take shorthand, but I spoke good English and had the youthful bravura to claim that I could do anything and everything.

The fact that I was never a member of the Hitler Youth and was the granddaughter of a Jew put me in a position of trust within the organization. In those early post-war days, the CIC was principally concerned with de-Nazification. The job of the agents assigned to the office in Salzburg was to catch Nazis and war criminals and turn them over to higher authority for punishment.

I became the principal interpreter during interrogations of suspected war criminals and through my own connections within the refugee camps in Salzburg was instrumental in the arrest of a high Gestapo official from Iglau, my home town.

I became as avid a Nazi hunter as those American agents, but I also was able to correct some wrong assumptions.

The agents used a manual on the hierarchy and titles of the Third Reich. Anyone with the title of "Hofrat," this manual stated, should be arrested. Hofrat is a title that was prevalent in the Austro-Hungarian Empire and means "adviser to the Court." It was still used in a bureaucratic way during World War II, but most people with the title were former civil servants of the Empire and quite elderly. They had nothing to do with the Nazi regime and were utterly bewildered when brought in for interrogation.

Needless to say, "Hofrat" was taken off the list of suspects.

Our agents did catch a big fish in the early spring of 1946. We had been advised that an infamous SS official in the Mauthausen concentration camp was hiding on a nearby farm in the guise of a polish refugee. When he was arrested, the farmer's wife pleaded with the Americans not to take him away. Her husband was still missing in Russia, and the suspected man had become invaluable to her, caring for the animals, loving her children. He could not possibly hurt a fly, she kept insisting.

Interrogation at CIC headquarters revealed him to be the cold-blooded murderer he was.

There were times when I had to leave the room, because my interpretations had become emotional and incoherent. I had not thought it possible that a human being could confess so dispassionately to the most heinous crimes. The man was turned over to a War Crimes Tribunal and was later hanged.

By the end of 1946 or spring of 1947, de-Nazification became no longer the sole preoccupation of the CIC. Relations between Russia and the U.S. had cooled and there was less cooperation and more political tension.

We had a Soviet Mission in Salzburg, ostensibly to persuade Russian refugees in the camps to return to Russia. Their main purpose, however, was to spy on the American forces in the U.S. sector of Austria.

I remember long dinner parties (at which, for no reason that I can remember, I was included) at the Russian Mission. With the caviar came endless vodka toasts to Russia, to the U.S.A., to every person present, all designed to get the Americans as drunk as possible and perhaps elicit some unguarded remark or better, have them fall under the table to be carried out by the Russian hosts who, in doing so, would try to rifle their pockets.

To this day I have an aversion to vodka, because, even if one surreptitiously poured most of it under the table, enough had to be consumed to make one rather ill.

An incident, long since declassified, brought an end to the Russian presence in Salzburg. I was working late with my boss one evening, when a call came from one of the agents who was secluded in a safe house with a man he was debriefing. He reported suspicious sightings around the house and asked for the dispatch of some MPs (military police) to check the premises.

When the MPs arrived, they found and arrested half a dozen Russians in U.S. military police uniforms trying to kidnap the man our agent was debriefing. Needless to say, that was the end of the Russian Mission in the American Zone of Occupation.

With the growing East-West tensions came a new directive from Washington that "indigenous" personnel could no longer handle "secret information." I was relegated back to the steno pool and decided that it was time to move on. I left my job at CIC in April, 1947.

Life in Post-War Salzburg

With a job that paid better wages than most Austrians made, a room with a wonderful family and enough to eat, I felt content, although often beset with homesickness for my parents and Altenberg. There was no way for us to visit them, but we still hoped to be able to return soon. In the meantime one lived in the present. Whenever I could, I would visit the Honsig farm in Henndorf, to see my sister and to help with harvest or daily chores.

The Austrian population had become quite used to the "Amis," as the Americans were called. The military government was trying hard to help Salzburg get back on its feet.

In the summer of 1946, the first post-war Music Festival was staged. "Jedermann" was once again performed in front of the cathedral and noted opera singers and musicians appeared from nowhere to perform in opera and concerts.

"No smoking" signs were posted by the Americans in the great Festival House. This created a small uproar in the local papers since "smoking" means "black tie" in German; they assumed "black tie" had been banned from the Festival House. An amusing story now, but at the time it showed how little the population understood about their conquerors.

The apartment where I lived did not have a bathroom with a tub or shower. All I had was a washstand in my room and access to hot water in the kitchen. A girlfriend told me she simply would walk into one of the big hotels, now occupied by officers of the U.S. Army. She knew the hotel from pre-war days and would head straight for the bathroom, lock herself in, take a long leisurely bath and then depart again as quietly as possible. Of course, one had to be careful not to be caught. I thought that a splendid idea and still remember the absolute bliss of a hot bath! I too, was never caught.

My social life was based more and more on American friends. Austrians were still struggling and few men of my age had come back from the war. So it became easy to enjoy the parties given by one's colleagues at the office, to eat in the Officer's Mess, drink wine and whiskey and to dance to American jazz and listen to Frank Sinatra.

I remember a big party that the French Mission in Salzburg gave for General Lawton Collins, the "Liberator'" of Salzburg. It was held in a large villa in Reichenhall, just over the border in Germany and my CIC colleagues led the convoy of cars and cleared everyone through the border.

The party required "evening dress" for the ladies and black tie or dress uniform for the men. I agonized for days about a dress. A niece of my landlady finally loaned me a pre-World War II dress with matching shoes and a piece of fur. I felt quite special in all that finery, although the shoes pinched dreadfully.

We were greeted at the door by the French hosts and my sister, who knew the owners of the house and in their absence acted as their representative. Marietta looked absolutely beautiful in a dress that must have come from Paris and was the envy of every woman in the room.

As the evening progressed, General Collins, who had entertained himself and us by playing the drums in the orchestra, decided to dance with every girl in the room. When my turn came, he asked me who I was and when I told him I was Marietta's sister, he held me away from him, looked me over and announced: "What a shame to play ugly duckling to such a beautiful swan."

Needless to say, I never forgave the General for that remark. I never saw him again either. He later divorced his wife, married his Salzburg girlfriend, and after he retired moved permanently to Salzburg where he died and is buried. Tourists are shown his grave in the beautiful graveyard of St. Peter. I have stood there many times, telling the stone that marks his grave how cruel I thought his remark had been that night.

One day in the summer of 1946, I was asked by my co-workers at CIC if I would like to go to Dachau, the former concentration camp. I knew a lot more than I did during the war about the horror of these camps, but I was not prepared for the shock of being confronted with the evidence of the mass murders committed there.

This was a time when ordinary citizens, especially students, were urged and sometimes forced to go through the camp and to see with their own eyes what crimes against humanity the Third Reich had committed.

The camp had not yet been organized into the memorial it is today. The impact was therefore even more profound. One could see on the faces of the people the shock the sights evoked. We drove back to Salzburg in total silence, each one of us struggling to absorb what we had seen. Catching Nazis and bringing them to justice became, more than ever, our mission.

Since few Austrians owned a car at that time, we used bicycles for covering great distances. I was quite used to biking 20 or 30 kms. just to go swimming in one of the lakes of the Salzkammergut on a summer's day. We would bicycle out to the Untersberg mountain, climb the mountain, run back down and cycle back home. I was twenty years old and in great physical shape.

During the next few years, I held several interesting jobs with the Occupation Forces. I worked for the Public Welfare Division which was sponsoring a lunch program for Austrian school children. The Trapp Family sent an enormous amount of CARE packages which we received and distributed. I remember inspecting orphanages which I would leave sobbing after spending time with little children who would wind their arms around my neck, asking with anxious, sad eyes "Mami? Mami?"

After one year with the Public Welfare Division, I switched to another division called the Austrian Youth Activities Program. That job was really fun.

The object of the military government was to make sure that the children of Salzburg would not be lured into activities sponsored by the Communist Party. We put on Soap Box Derby races, sponsored a Golden Glove boxing tournament and rented a castle outside of Salzburg, where needy children spent a blissful summer with good nourishment and plenty of outdoor activities. I learned a lot about boxing, as I had to arrange the Golden Glove tournaments and had to climb into the rink to proclaim the winners.

My boss was a First Lieutenant who spent most of his day with his feet propped up on his desk reading racy paperback novels. One day a delegation of portly Salzburg gentlemen arrived and asked to speak to the "Herr Leutnant." They would not tell me why, but wanted to speak to him in private.

After about 20 minutes my boss burst out of his office, almost apoplectic with suppressed laughter. The gentlemen had asked for his help in putting on a special festival up on the "Festung," the castle above Salzburg, for the many orphans. But what they wanted, were a thousand or even just a few hundred CONDOMS, which they would dye pink, blue and yellow and blow up into balloons. It could be done, they assured him earnestly; they had successfully created oblong balloons. It was a clever idea, as balloons were unavailable at that time in Austria. However, as my boss pointed out, as Youth Activities Officer he could not possibly requisition condoms. He would surely be fired; he could even be court marshaled!

The gentlemen left very disappointed. After they left, we began to think. Could we put signs into the various latrines used by the soldiers, asking for contributions? Would my lieutenant become the laughing stock of Salzburg if he did that? We contemplated distributing leaflets asking for contributions. I no longer recall the exact sequence of events, but in the end, the festival for the orphans had balloons, nice little oblong balloons that the children, starved for toys, loved.

My last job before my own immigration was with the Displaced Persons Division. I acted as interpreter during hundreds of interviews conducted by the Immigration Officers of persons from Hungary, Russia, Rumania, etc. These were people whose homes had disappeared behind the Iron Curtain and who were eager to start a new life in America. Many of them were Jews, people who had survived the camps where their families had perished. The stories were heartbreaking and we all worked hard to help these people fill out the necessary documents that would make them eligible for immigration.

In 1948, after the Communist takeover of Czechoslovakia, my parents also arrived in Austria. They had signed over the entire estate as a gift to the Czech Government for the permission to leave legally. We obtained permission from the Provisional Austrian Government and the Four-Power Occupation Forces for them to enter Austria. They had survived the Russian occupation and three more years of increasing uncertainty until they finally realized that there would be no future for us in Czechoslovakia under the Communist regime.

They arrived in Salzburg in a van that held the pathetic remnants of a once-proud and beautiful home. They were allowed to take nothing of value, none of the antiques, silver, paintings or oriental rugs—only the bedding off all the beds, down pillows, down comforters, sheets and blankets and lots of kitchen furniture some china and pots and pans. All that down proved of great value for a while, as they sold most of it for welcome cash until they got settled.

My father worked as a forester on an estate for a while, my mother as companion to an ancient Italian princess. Eventually, the Austrian government settled a small pension on my father as a World War I hero. My parents moved to Vienna, taking with them my younger sister who had been separated from them for three long years.

Skiing and Love for the Mountains

Ever since I was a child, I loved the mountains. I would lie flat on my back in the grass and look at the clouds above me. I would imagine them to be the Himalayas and depending on the book I was reading, it would be Everest, or Nanga Parbat or perhaps Switzerland with the Matterhorn if the cloud resembled that distinctive mountain. As a teenager I did not miss any of the great Leni-Riefenstahl/Louis Trenker movies, movies of love and betrayal in the mountains.

The first thing I did, when we reached Henndorf and the farm was to walk up to the highest point behind the farm and gaze towards Salzburg and the snow-covered peaks.

However, it was not until travel became easier and I could take a train to Kitzbühel in the Tyrolean Alps that I began to REALLY ski.

A sister of my father had married a widower who was a respected lawyer in Kitzbühel and in the 1970s became one of the best and most innovative mayors the town ever had. Both were no longer young and had no children. They invited me to come and visit anytime I could get away from Salzburg.

Tante Emy was a bit of a snob, determined to "launch" me into the society of Kitzbühel with the ultimate goal of an appropriate marriage. In the meantime she taught me how to ski. She skied on very long skis in the style of the 1920s, loved speed and powder snow and knew everyone in town, from ski instructor to castle owner.

The true bond between us however, was a shared love for the mountains. Some of my best memories are of either skiing or hiking with her.

In 1947, there was still a scarcity of fresh eggs, butter and "speck," the smoke-cured bacon that is a staple of a farmer's diet. Tante Emy and I would hike up the mountains to remote farm houses to buy these delicacies. She would always know who had the best "speck" or had just made the best schnapps. We would return late in the afternoon, our rucksacks heavy with freshly-baked bread, eggs, butter, speck and schnapps. Along the way she would point out the mountains in the distance, name every peak and teach me about wildflowers by the wayside.

She taught me how to snowplow and make snowplow turns, but I mostly learned by following her or other people. On a sunny March morning, in the days before Kitzbühel became a network of lifts, we would take the first cable car up to the Hahnenkamm, and walk to a point that offered a particular steep run down into the valley. Then we would wait till the sun had softened the snow to a perfect 2cm corn snow surface and launch ourselves down virgin slopes, past little "alm" huts till we finally came into the woods and found a road.

We would knock at the first farm house—Tante Emy, of course, knew the owners—and we would beg a hearty breakfast. We would look back up the mountain and see our faint tracks in the snow. Never again, with all the skiing I have done since, have I experienced such perfect bliss.

My uncle wanted me to move to Kitzbühel and work for him. Instead, I immigrated to America. I have often wondered what would have happened had I stayed. I am sure Tante Emy would have married me off to some titled landowner in no time at all.

More Mountain Lore

In the early 1950s, ski equipment looked quite different from the down suits and jackets and the footwear of foam-filled inner-boots and plastic outer shells worn today.

Two boot makers were the rage of Austria in my early ski days. Mr. Haderer in Kitzbühel and Mr. Strolz in Lech am Arlberg. Both made custom-made leather boots, beautifully crafted with inner and outer laces and quite indestructible. Ladies wore stirrup stretch pants that were tucked into the boot. This assured the absolute stretch of the pants. They sat on one's hip, as I well remember and pulled downward giving the wearer a permanent back and stomach ache. You could not bend your knees, so sitting down became a backward leaning slouch, and tying boot-laces was sheer agony. You also had to be extremely careful that the pants folded cleanly around your ankles, many a time did I experience anklebones rubbed raw from a crease in those infernal pants.

We wore heavy wool sweaters and lightweight anoraks made of a tightly woven gabardine. Windproof, yes, but not warm. We had wool mittens that became stiff frozen boards if they got wet. All in all however, I do not remember ever feeling really cold, I suppose because we kept continually in motion.

Our skis were, of course, made out of wood. They had steel edges, but you were always careful to store your skis properly so that they would not warp. We waxed our skis daily—wax for cold weather, wax for warm weather, sometimes an application of both in anticipation of changing temperatures and snow conditions. You always carried wax with you, to reapply if necessary. Bindings consisted of cables that could be tightened for proper downhill control, or loosened for walking.

Since we knew little about the damage caused by skin exposure to high-altitude sun, we applied sun oil and got sunburned and peeled frequently. A deep tan was considered the ultimate in beautiful looks, however, and we would spend hours exposing as much of our bodies as was permissible to the tanning business.

I did not have much money in those days, and in order to acquire the proper equipment, I hired myself out to the Austrian cross-country team as a "girl Friday" for a new pair of skis and proper boots. I would join the team on weekends wherever they trained, wax their skis (a lot of the wax was applied using a hot iron), sew on buttons, press their clothes and after watching the masseur, do some light massaging. They were a wonderful crew of men and women and one of my rewards was to be part of the support team during races, to hand out pieces of orange or a drink of water on the course and to be part of the celebrations afterwards.

In late April some of us would prepare to hike up to a glacier for some late spring skiing. The closest glacier to Salzburg was the Kitzsteinhorn, near the village of Zell am See. In 1949, there were no cable cars to take you up to the glacier and there was only a simple hut one could use for overnight shelter. You took a train to Zell am See and a post bus to the hamlet of Kaprun and then started walking.

To get up to the hut took about six hours. First you hiked up through the woods carrying your skis, and as soon as you got above the tree line and into snow, you put on "skins," and made your way up between the rocks and boulders. The "skins" I am speaking of were strips of seal skin which, properly attached to the underside of your skis, would prevent you from sliding backwards. The hairs of the seal skin would act as brakes.

In addition to gear and food for two days, everyone carried a couple of pieces of firewood to present to the "Huettenwirt"—the keeper of the hut.

Slowly gaining altitude, we would traverse to the right, then turn to the left and traverse, and repeat this pattern endlessly for hours. If the day was sunny, we would get very hot with all that exertion and after a while it became harder and harder not to stop too often to take a sip of water or eat a piece of chocolate or fruit. You could see the hut when you were still quite far below it. "Hallelujah," you would think, "We are there at last," only to have the hut disappear behind a rock for another interminable time period.

Once at the hut, we would collapse, exhausted but happy to be there. Hot tea with lots of sugar would revive us and we would be ready for the fun and companionship of life in a mountain hut and the food we all shared. We went to bed early on simple mattresses with the pillows and blankets provided by our host.

The next morning we rose early, while it was still dark, and again attaching skins to our skis would follow the "Huettenwirt" up the glacier to the foot of the summit pyramid. Leaving the skis in the snow, we would scramble up to the top for a glorious view of the world below us, deep blue shadows on the glacier and peaks all around us touched pink by the rising sun.

Once again on the glacier, we would put on our skis and, careful to stay in the tracks of our guide, ski down the untracked, pristine white glacier, back to the hut. After a hearty breakfast, we would gather our gear and head back down into the valley. We would ski as far as we could, and shoulder our skis once we came to the end of the snow and the woods below. Catching the local bus and train back to Salzburg we would arrive tired, sunburned but bursting with pride that we had climbed, conquered and skied the Kitzsteinhorn.

I have been back to the Kitzsteinhorn many times since those days. They now have state-of-the-art cable cars to take you up the mountain in two stages that help to acclimatize you. The glacier itself is crisscrossed with lifts and at the foot of the summit pyramid the lift terminates into a large station, where you find full restaurant amenities.

I am glad that I was able to experience the majesty of that world before technology intruded; where only the wind and an occasional piece of snow rolling down slope broke the stillness, and where one was just a tiny speck in a vast, white expanse.

Immigration

The outbreak of the Korean War had brought new anxiety to Europe. Could this war escalate into another World War?

At that time, a family friend who now lived in New York came through Salzburg and took me out to dinner. We talked about world affairs and my anxieties. Otto Kallir was in Austria to lecture about Grandma Moses, the old lady from Vermont who had taken up painting when she could no longer do fine stitching. He had discovered her a few years earlier and her simple paintings of farm life in Vermont had become the rage of America.

Otto offered to sponsor me if I wanted to come to America. I could stay with his family and even make myself useful by typing the manuscript of the book he was writing about Grandma Moses.

I mulled his offer over for weeks—the more I thought about it, the more appealing the thought became. After working for the American Occupation Forces for six years I felt an affinity for the American way of life and, besides, the adventure of immigration appealed to me.

I went to Vienna and asked my parents' advice. They were not enamored with the idea. Only a black sheep of the family had immigrated in the last century to America, never to be heard of again. I told them I would be safe staying with the Kallirs and besides, I would have to pass all kinds of examinations before I would be accepted as a "displaced person applying for immigration". The latter proved to be easier and faster than even I thought. After receiving the affidavit of sponsorship from Otto Kallir, I sailed through the health check, political check and inquiries about my moral standing in the community.

In March of 1951, I was still working for the Displaced Persons Commission and saw the OK clearance before anyone else. It was a

Friday and I had planned to go skiing for a few days. I hid my file and went off to the mountains.

When I came back, I was told by my boss that he had found my file and had activated it, and that I was scheduled to leave for Bremerhaven and debarkation in two weeks.

The final decision was thus made for me. I went to Vienna to say good-bye to my family.

My mother gave me a set of 12 of the silver-plated cutlery that they had been able to bring out of Czechoslovakia (each piece had the seven-pronged crown engraved above the initials of my parents). She thought that might help my social standing in America!

I packed a trunk with my meager belongings and began to say good-bye to my friends. By 1951, my circle of friends had changed completely. I had become an avid skier and most of the people I knew were as enamored by mountains and skiing as I was.

Besides leaving behind my family, I found it difficult to say good-bye to the beautiful countryside of Salzburg especially my beloved mountains.

When the day finally came, I boarded the train, clutching a bunch of daffodils. I watched my friends in the station disappearing through the haze of my tears, and then I really broke down when the Untersberg and the rest of the Salzburg mountains came into view. Would I ever see them again? A kind conductor on the train, witnessing my distress, tried to comfort me while I sobbed on his shoulder

The trip to Bremerhaven took 24 hours, but with my usual resilience, I soon concentrated on the scenery and made new friends. The closer we got to northern Germany the more evident the destruction of the war became. In Bremen I remember seeing the statue of the "Eiserner Roland," but most buildings were still in ruins, or in early stages of re-building.

In Bremerhaven, all the people on the train joined other immigrants in a large camp. As I remember, we slept on straw and were given two blankets each. We must have been fed three times a day, but I have only a hazy recollection of the 10 days or perhaps two weeks we spent in Bremerhaven. I met many people I had processed during my workdays at the Displaced Persons Commission. Word got around that I was at the camp and these people would come to thank me for helping them to be on their way to freedom and America. They would bring little gifts, chocolate or a jar of jam. I was quite overwhelmed—after all, I had only done my duty.

I also befriended a Hungarian countess with the illustrious name of Esterhazy. What a change it was for her, from castles and great wealth in Hungary to the straw pallets of the immigration camp. Her sister had already gone to America and now it was her turn to join her.

Finally the day came when we were told to board the ship. I don't know what I had expected, but when I saw this little gray ship sitting low in the water I was quite appalled. The 12,000 ton S.S. General Sturgis had been a troop transport ship during the war. The Captain and the crew were American, and the officials dealing with the immigrants were part of the International Rescue Commission.

Since I had very little luggage, I had decided to bring my skis. I also owned a beautiful fur-lined coat which a tailor in Salzburg had made for me. The tailor had known my family in Prague when he was one of the best tailors in Czechoslovakia, and out of love for my parents had made me this coat for very little money. I must have been quite a sight coming up the gangplank, wearing a handsome coat, a rucksack on my back, a hat on my head (my mother had insisted that I would enter the U.S.A. with a proper hat) and carrying a pair of skis.

At the top of the gangplank stood a gentleman who looked like something out of Gilbert & Sullivan. He wore a splendid uniform with ribbons, highly-polished boots, fierce mustaches and sideburns and was holding a swagger stick. He looked very important so I decided on the spur of the moment to make myself noticed. I rammed my skis into his middle pretending to stumble and then apologized profusely in my best "British" English.

He simply waved me on with his swagger stick and I descended into the bowels of the ship where I was assigned a hammock in a vast chamber with perhaps 100 other women. We dined that night, as we would for the rest of the journey, standing at long hanging tables side by side, row after row, as the food was served to us on metal plates.

That night we crossed the English Channel in very rough weather. Every one was seasick or so I thought as I heard and smelled the vomiting women. I decided I would NOT get seasick, so for all the hours it took to cross the channel, I pretended to ski. When we pitched, I skied the bumps; when we rolled sideways, I waited for the next pitch.

In the morning I had marks in the palms of my hands where I had dug my nails, determined not to have to get out of my hammock. The morning revealed a sorry sight—vomit everywhere with groaning and crying women lying in their hammocks.

I had to do something to get out of that hold. I went in search of the fearsome looking Englishman. When I found him, I again apologized to him, told him of the situation in the women's cabin and offered my services as a secretary/interpreter. He immediately hired me—gave me a clipboard to write down his comments and off we went to inspect the boat.

In the hold for the women, he asked for volunteers to get the women out of their hammocks and up onto the deck and to organize a clean-up brigade. I learned that all the work on the ship that had to do with the immigrants would be done by them. Work details were already being formed. It quickly emerged that the well-educated, the so-called upper class passengers, were the ones who rallied to do the work. Many of the people afflicted with seasickness simply gave in and wallowed in their misery and it was up to a few to rouse them and force them to help themselves. By the end of the first day, a semblance of order had been established.

My mentor, as it turned out, had been a Colonel in the British Army who came out of retirement to help the resettlement of refugees. He was a Scotsman and when we finally sailed past the cliffs of Dover, he put on his kilt and took out his bagpipes and marched up and down on the deck saluting his country. It was a wonderful sight and quite a spectacle for most of us who had never heard the sound of bagpipes.

After two nights in the hold with so many women, I asked the Colonel if he could not find other sleeping arrangements for me. The dear man did. Opposite the hospital was a cabin with bunks for three nurses, but only two nurses occupied it, so I very gratefully moved in.

I never got seasick, and as we chugged along across the Atlantic Ocean I began to enjoy life on board ship. It was like Noah's Ark, a ship full of people of different ethnic and social background and speaking many different languages.

Men slept in different holds from the women and women with children had cabins. This seemed to be especially hard on the Jewish fathers who wanted to be with their families. We constantly received complaints from women who found the husbands of other women in the cabin with them. The husbands, when confronted, accused the complaining woman (if she was not Jewish) of anti-Semitism, which in turn brought the rabbi to ask for a formal hearing at the "kangaroo" court. The "kangaroo court" convened every evening and consisted of the Captain of the ship, the Colonel, the ship's doctor and a chosen representative from the passengers.

Complaints could be brought before this court and judgment had to be accepted. The complaints were varied and often hilarious. A Hungarian and a Rumanian almost killed each other over a few meters of land that each claimed as his country's soil. People stole items from each other or accused people of stealing. A woman one evening accused another woman of wearing her precious silk panties. One of the work details complained that their leader had visions of past grandeur. The elderly man had been an officer during World War I and now happily drilled his work detail as though they were foot soldiers. There were complaints about the food—perfectly edible Navy chow, but foreign to some of these simple people.

The worst problem arose towards the end of the voyage. A whole delegation of rabbis came to announce that the Passover wine they were carrying with them had disappeared. Grave consequences were to be expected if the ship did not reach New York before Passover. This was a crisis the Captain did not want to confront. The ship chugged on a bit faster and we did get to New York just in time.

I will never forget my first glimpse of New York. We arrived at night and all the skyscrapers looked like jewels in the night sky. The famous Statue of Liberty was lit up in greeting—it gave you goose pimples but also made you realize that the voyage was over, that we had arrived and that we would soon have to confront a new life in a new country.

Because of the crisis with the Passover wine, we were cleared through quarantine faster than usual and in no time we filed off the boat to be greeted by a medical team in white coats who liberally doused us with DDT. It was the 20th of April, 1951.

General MacArthur had been honored during a parade that day and it took some time for the Kallirs to pick me up at the pier. While I waited, sitting on my trunk, hat on my head and clutching my skis, members of the New York press walked among us immigrants, interviewing people here and there. When they came up to me, I told them that I had brought my skis in the hope of being able to ski in this magnificent country. The next day I read in the paper that the "American taxpayer was picking up the tab for young woman who looked prosperous and seemed to have come on an immigration boat so that she could ski...."

That was the only time I made a New York newspaper.

Early Life in New York

Unlike my friend, the Hungarian countess who started her life in New York right away with a job as a nanny, I moved in with the Kallirs, who had a spacious apartment on Riverside Drive.

The Kallirs' daughter was studying in Vienna and I was given her room with a private bath—I was in seventh heaven. One can imagine my mortification, when I discovered that despite the liberal spraying with DDT upon debarkation, I was full of head lice. Although the remedies available were a lot less painful than the petroleum cure of my early childhood, I nonetheless felt like a leper and spent days ridding myself of that scourge.

Otto Kallir had progressed with the writing of the Grandma Moses book and I very soon settled into a routine of typing his manuscript. I was rather timid about getting out to explore New York. It was so big and loud and busy with traffic that I welcomed the chance to stay home and type in a pretty, sun-filled room with a glorious view of the Hudson River.

Otto Kallir took me to the gallery he owned on 57th Street and as we walked along Fifth Avenue and turned west on 57th Street, I marveled at how different people looked. Elderly women seemed to share a preference for pink and pale blue suits and wore the most interesting hats, with lots of fruit—cherries and grapes—decorating the basic hat. I had never seen anything like it. And every woman, young and old, wore little white gloves. The men wore Homburgs which seemed so much more formal than what I was used to.

I was dazzled by the display of finery in the shop windows and by the food markets that sold everything from meat to fruit. I was still used to individual shops—one for meat, another for dairy products and another for fruit, etc. The skyscrapers overwhelmed me.

Grandma Moses came to New York to speak to a women's group at the Waldorf-Astoria.

She was a wonderful old lady, quite shopworn and bent-over, but sharp as a tack.

On the main stage, with the curtains drawn, someone asked her if she was not afraid to face "that sea of women out there …" "Not at all," she said with a twinkle in her eyes. "They sound just like the chickens in my chicken coop back home".

In addition to typing for Otto Kallir, I also tried to make contact with some of the people to whom I had recommendations.

One day, a couple of years earlier in Salzburg, a young man had walked into my office and asked if he could get a job for a few weeks. It seemed that he was to meet his brother in Salzburg, but till he did, he had no money left. The brothers had toured Europe together but separated when one wanted to hit the high spots in Austria and the other wanted to experience solitude in the mountains. Love for mountains was all I had to hear from the young man. I could not offer him a job, but I took him home with me, fed him a decent meal and put him up at a small hotel where I vouched for his ability to pay.

A few days later the brother appeared and both went back to the states impressing upon me that if I ever came to New York I should look them up. I even received a very sweet note from their mother thanking me for my hospitality.

So I called them and found myself very quickly adopted by this very hospitable and warmhearted family. The young man whom I had fed in Salzburg was at that point living in Washington D.C., but the other one was a young lawyer in New York and about to get married. I was included in prenuptial parties, met a lot of young people who in turn asked me to spend weekends at their parents' country houses and attended the huge wedding at one of the big New York churches. I had an introduction to a stratum of New York society which, as a European living with a European family, I could never have had a chance of meeting.

I was impressed with how easily and naturally these people accepted me and took me into their homes. In Europe it would take ages before one would be invited to spend a night with people one had just met. Naturally, I was a bit intimidated—all this wealth and all these new friends so carefree and unencumbered by the weight of history. But I resolved not to compare, not to talk too much about where I had come from and who I was. There was no way I could compete, so I just thanked them for their gracious hospitality and took this new world at face value.

When the Kallirs decided to spend the summer in Europe, Otto called his good friend the Baroness Trapp in Stowe, Vt. to see if she needed someone to help run their annual summer music camp. She did, and I soon found myself on the way to Vermont to spend the summer.

It was July of 1951 and I immediately fell in love with Vermont with its woods, quaint villages and mountains. The Trapp lodge was not as grand as it is today. It was a big, comfortable house constantly undergoing construction to add a room here and a passageway there.

By the time I met the family, the Baron had died. I am not even sure that the family still sang for a living. The Baroness had just published the book about their flight from Austria but the musical "The Sound of Music" was still a long way off.

Of the original offspring of the Baron, only one son, and three of the girls were still living at the farm. There were, of course, the three younger children, Lori, Rosemary and Johannes. In addition there was Father Wasner, the priest who had followed them into exile and had also become their musical director.

I was supposed to help as sort of a "girl Friday" with the summer camp, run on a schedule of turnover every two weeks. The camp was situated in the woods below the main house. A former Army training camp, it consisted of many wood cabins housing six to eight people in twin cubicles, a mess hall with a fully equipped kitchen, and a chapel with an altar and benches for people to sit on.

The family had bought the structures from the Army after the war and had furnished the cabins in the "Austrian" style, with red-and-white checkered curtains, sheets and tablecloths. The furniture was simple, some of it custom-made, some of it purchased in thrift shops or donated by friends. A beautiful wood-carved pieta, imported from Austria, was the main attraction on the altar. The Trapp family was very religious and most of the people who attended the camp were Catholic. They came to play the recorder or other musical instruments, to find refuge from the stress of daily life and to mingle with the members of the most famous Catholic family in America. There were nuns on holiday retreat, lonely hearts who found peace and companionship and many priests who came for a week or so to pray and find inspiration in talking with the Baroness and Father Wasner.

"Mutter" Trapp, as we all called her, was definitely the heart and soul of daily life in camp. She organized outings and parlor games and with her flair for the dramatic made daily vespers an unforgettable event. Candles adorned the walls of the "chapel" and after the service held by Father Wasner, the family would sing while acolytes extinguished one candle after the other till only the husky solo alto of "Mutter" Trapp could be heard.

She held "fireside chats" without the fire in her cabin, devoted to her interpretation of the New Testament with general discussion on the subject following her lecture. People had a wonderful time, especially the nuns and priests, whom she would take on rough cross-country rides in her Jeep.

I must admit, although I was not a devout Catholic, I had a good time. There was an air of childish innocence connected with the camp which was a welcome respite from the more serious aspects of life in general.

Mutter Trapp was, of course, no paragon of saintly kindness. She was a ruthless promoter of the Trapp Family and herself and all the children suffered at one point or other under the yoke she imposed upon them. However, she did make them famous and with the proceeds from their singing, the family helped many people in Salzburg after the war. It is an irony of fate that by selling the rights to her book, she was cut out of the millions the musical and film have made. Only on the periphery did the family profit from it all.

At the end of the summer, Mrs. Trapp asked me to become her secretary. I declined. I was not cut out for a life of pious adoration of "Mutter" Trapp.

Instead, I got myself a job with the Mt. Mansfield Company. The general manager of the company was an Austrian from Linz who hired me as an assistant to his secretary. "Maxi," as she was known to everyone, was a wonderful character, devoted to her boss and her job. She held a lot of responsibilities and was a hard taskmaster—but one with a heart of gold.

Most of the employees were housed in cramped quarters under the big cafeteria. I shared a room with one of the seasonal chambermaids. All the ski instructors were billeted in rooms for two or even four to a room, but nobody cared—we had a lot of fun. Two former racers from Austria were in Stowe that winter as instructors and several of the gold medal winners of the Oslo Olympics joined us later that winter.

Stowe can be terribly cold in the winter and since I had an office job, I could only take the "milk run" every morning with some of the instructors, a toe- and finger-numbing exercise. Those were the days before Gore-Tex and down outer wear—we were cold! I used to wrap newspaper around my socks to create more insulation before I pulled on my leather boots.

At the end of winter, the company offered me a summer job. I thought about it because I liked Stowe and the many friends I had made there. But in the end I went back to New York to look for better job opportunities.

For a while I stayed with a friend who had a great apartment around the corner from the Metropolitan Museum of Art. She worked at the museum but did not have to be there until 10 a.m. In lieu of rent, I had to make breakfast every morning and bring it to her in bed, while she read the papers or worked. It was a most satisfactory arrangement and gave me time to look for a job.

Marriage Years

I found a job as a receptionist at a public relations firm on Madison Avenue near 42nd Street. I do not remember much about my duties, but I do remember that the company would throw a cocktail party to celebrate any occasion such as the birthday of an executive or a secretary.

At the end of the work day, caterers would appear to set up the boardroom with liquor and hors d'oeuvres, and all the secretaries would withdraw to the ladies room to refresh their makeup, even change their clothes. At 5:30 the fun would begin. It would be a drink-fest with hilarity and familiarity where secretaries became sirens and the middle aged executives became macho conquerors. This was long before sexual harassment suits, and although I never participated in these festivities, I also never heard complaints afterwards.

I had met Tom Mason, my future husband, shortly after I returned to New York. We were married in June of 1952.

Tom was a lawyer with a well-known New York law firm. In those days one joined a law firm right out of law school and expected to spend the rest of one's life with that firm, slowly climbing the ladder from associate to senior associate to junior partner and senior partner and perhaps some day head of the firm. The "firm" became your family, looked after you in time of need, and in turn expected complete loyalty from you.

Tom had been a brilliant student at Yale College and continued at Yale Law School where he graduated third in his class and won several high honors. He had barely started to work when he went off to fight in World War II, leaving behind a young wife and son. He was part of the brutal Battle of the Bulge and came back to the U.S. somewhat shell-shocked and began to drink heavily. He and his wife had another son, but eventually divorced. When I met Tom in the spring of 1952, he was a bachelor and not drinking at all.

I was 26 years old and ready to get married. Tom was nine years older and more mature than any the young men I had met so far. I was dazzled by his mind, his erudition and his knack to play "devil's advocate" in almost every discussion and on every subject, which appealed to me.

He, in turn, was drawn to my sunny and down-to-earth disposition. The fact that I came from a different country and social background did not matter; he dismissed it as unimportant. However, differences in habits of daily living, nuances of opinions and fundamental beliefs surfaced quickly and I do remember how I struggled to adjust. Those were the days when wives yielded to their husbands. The age of equality of the sexes within marriage had not yet dawned.

We found a nice apartment on East 72nd Street and 2nd Avenue. Tom bought one of the first Volkswagens to be sold in this country—a white cabriolet—and on weekends we drove up to Madison, Conn., where his mother had a small house.

When I think back, I marvel how my mother-in-law welcomed a foreign daughter-in-law with open arms. She put up with us every weekend, and during holidays and summer vacations, Tom's two boys came to stay with her as well. This, in addition to her two daughters who also came to spend weekends, especially in the summer when Madison offered Long Island Sound and a lively summer community. She cooked and sewed for us and put load after load of our clothes through her washing machine while we played tennis or enjoyed the beach. She never complained and was always welcoming and loving. She was an extremely practical and down-to-earth woman who could do anything she put her mind to. I wish she had lived longer than her eighty years. I not only admired and respected her, but at the end I truly loved her.

Our social life in New York revolved to a large degree around "the firm." Some of it was voluntary, while some of it involved "command performances" at the houses or lavish apartments of the senior partners. One year I was asked to be in charge of the annual Christmas party. This affair was a luncheon in a private downtown club. All the ladies received large corsages upon arrival and before one sat down to eat, one replenished one's drink of gin or bourbon or scotch, to sip during the meal.

Well, I changed all that. No more corsages. I used the budget at my disposal to serve Beluga caviar before lunch, shortened the cocktail hour and served a decent wine with lunch. I set a precedent, as in the 1950s few Americans drank wine with their meals.

In 1953, a year after my marriage, I had saved enough money through my current job, to pay for passage on a ship to Europe. Tom had urged me to do this, to build a bridge in my mind between the "Old World" and the "New World" and to realize that distances could be overcome.

I traveled on the Queen Elizabeth I, that grand old lady of a ship. I had a berth in the lowest class, but friends of ours were in first class and I managed to slip up there, usually at tea time, to gorge myself at a proper English tea. My return voyage was on the Liberte, formerly a German ship, then owned by the French. None of these ships still exists today, but I am glad that I was able to experience this much longer and slower form of crossing the Atlantic.

In Vienna, I felt very American, and constantly defended my new country from local criticism. Europeans in those days still considered America as uncivilized, a country where all food came out of cans and where making money was the sole purpose for living.

I was glad to see my parents and my sisters. My mother had adjusted marvelously to her new life. She had learned to cook—she became a very good cook—and bemoaned the fact that for so many years she had been at the mercy of her servants. My parents had bought an apartment through the sale of whatever valuables they still possessed and both my sister Marietta and my sister Christine lived with them. But my father was beginning to fade. He never did get over the loss of Altenberg and he hated the fact that he had to accept monetary help from his daughters. He became somewhat senile in the last years of his life, perhaps with little strokes, perhaps with the onset of Alzheimer's—I do not know. He died in 1957 at age sixty-nine. My mother lived until 1968. She was only seventy when she died.

Our son Christopher was born on May 20, 1958 at Lennox Hill Hospital in New York.

A couple of years later, we bought our own house in Madison, Conn., which we used for weekends and summer vacations. From the time of my marriage, Tom's sons, Thomas and Robin, stayed with us on holidays and during their long summer vacations. This was no hardship for me—I love children and enjoyed having them stay with us, first at Mother Mason's house and later at our own house. When I first met them, Thomas was about five years old and Robin was three. By the time Christopher came along, both boys were old enough to need less supervision and Robin, the younger one, was especially sweet with his half-brother.

Madison was a wonderful little town. Situated about 30 miles east of New Haven, directly on Long Island Sound, it was a sleepy village in the winter and a very lively one in the summer.

The "summer people" usually arrived at the end of June and departed on Labor Day. Their houses were those typical New England seaside wooden structures with large porches and windows, wicker furniture and old fashioned bathrooms. They were used for three months of the year and shut tight during the winter.

The house we bought was not directly on the water, but within sight of it. It was not a typical summer house, but an excellent copy of a New England cottage. Built by master craftsmen during the Depression, it had four bedrooms and two baths upstairs. The downstairs had wide oak floor boards, a beautiful beamed ceiling and a large fireplace. There were nice wrought iron details on doors and cupboards. We bought the house from friends, who sold it to us furnished. We just had to add a piece here and there. I especially remember the wonderful screened-in porch, the well-made porch furniture with deep green cushions and the smell of the jasmine bush that grew outside. The house had no cellar, and when we put in a heating system, we insulated the walls as well as we could. It was never meant to be a year-round house—we used it on weekends and in the summer.

Madison was famous up and down the seashore for its Beach Club. A "members only" club with a carefully selected membership (white, waspish and anti-Semitic), it was open from the last week of June through the weekend of Labor Day. The large clubhouse had a great ballroom with parquet floors and a stage at one end. There was a dining room, a large bar and a great covered porch open to the sea. A lawn sloped down to a beach. There were several bedrooms upstairs for guests of members. We did not have much of a harbor, so Madison never became a great sailing club, although there were small boats, mostly Sailfish, which raced against each other all summer. The Beach Club was, however, a very good tennis club. We had about six clay and two all-weather courts. There was a tennis pro and we all played a lot of tennis.

Summers in Madison revolved around the Beach Club. For the children there were many activities in and out of the water. We met on the beach, had lunch at the snack-bar, and at least once a week, we adults had cocktails on the porch followed by dinner in the dining room with a breathtaking view of the sunset on the water.

While the wives and children spent the entire summer in Madison, the husbands came on week-ends, from New York, New Jersey, or wherever they worked and the family lived during the rest of the year.

On Friday night, the wives would line up at the local train station to meet the New York train. The husbands, having had a jolly time in the bar car, would roll off the train, have a shower and change and be ready for the first of the many cocktail parties that were part of the summer week-ends.

The highlight on Saturday was the weekly dinner dance at the club. We ladies wore long dresses; the men wore tuxedos with the white summer jackets that were in fashion at the time. If one was not tired by midnight when the music stopped, one went on to other peoples' houses, ending up in the wee hours at someone's house for scrambled eggs.

The tennis players gathered for the Sunday morning "hangover round robin" which had to be followed by "Bloody Mary's" to kill the hangover. For Sunday lunch, we cooked huge 3-inch thick steaks on the grill, accompanied by fresh tomatoes and corn. The husbands went back to New York on Sunday night or early Monday morning, and we wives took a day or two to recover from the events of the weekend.

When I think back, we had a lot of fun, but drank too much, ate too much, and smoked too much.

Each August, the club put on a theatrical production, the "Madison Beach Club Follies," with a director and costumes provided by a professional company. The actors were the members of the club, from children to teenagers to the adult members. For about three weeks, everyone had a wonderful time rehearsing the various skits, and the fun culminated in two performances, one for the "townspeople" and one for members and guests only on Saturday night. The Follies were the highlight of the summer. Parents loved to see their children on stage and some of the adults put on memorable performances while others gamely kicked their legs in the chorus line or sang racy songs to the delight of the audience.

Another big event was the Fourth of July parade put on by the Madison Beach Club as a benefit for the "Fresh Air Fund". Along the beach road marched the high school band playing lustily, followed by the veterans in their uniforms waving large flags. Uncle Sam, resplendent in flag-draped top hat, sat in a large open touring car and bobbed and smiled and waved to the crowds. Following this group were all the children, in baby carriages and strollers, on tricycles and bicycles, dressed up in red, white and blue outfits and pushed and pulled by older siblings or their parents. The tricycles, bicycles and carriages were elaborately decorated in red-white-and blue streamers and colored crepe paper. Decorating these conveyances was a great ritual and lots of fun for the children.

The adults wore their best red white and blue outfits, some with matching hats. Everyone ended up on a large lawn, where Uncle Sam made a speech and ice cream was handed out to the children. Some of us adults shook collecting boxes at the onlookers and asked for donations. Each year we collected quite a bit of money for the "Fresh Air Fund".

To be free to participate in all these activities, we all had live-in babysitters to help with the children. In those days, it was possible to employ lovely young college girls through an agency that specialized in finding homes for girls who had become pregnant and were sent by their parents to another part of the country during their pregnancy, since abortion was not available or acceptable. The agency placed them into carefully selected families where they were paid pocket money, helped with chores and became part of the family. When their time came, the agency took them through their confinement. The babies were put out for adoption and the girls went back home to resume their lives. I had two girls one summer, lovely young women who were fun to have around and who were very responsible babysitters.

Christopher thrived in Madison. He loved the beach, the sand and the many children that were part of our summer community. But he also did not mind going back to New York. He loved the apartment in New York and going to Central Park to play. He was a well-adjusted and extremely adaptable little boy.

My mother came to America when Christopher was born, eager to meet her first grandchild, and I took Christopher to Austria in 1961when he was three years old. I rented a house on a lake in Carinthia and Chris, my mother and I had a wonderful time exploring the countryside and Christopher and my mother got to know each other.

In 1965, Tom's firm sent us to Paris, where Tom was to work in the firm's Paris office. Tom had been made a partner and life should have been going along well for us except that Tom was again drinking heavily. It was thought that sending him abroad, along with his family, would be beneficial. With less stress and more time for his family he might pull himself together. Unfortunately, this was not to be.

We had a very difficult time in Paris and he was sent back to New York after a mere six months. Christopher was the only one who truly benefited from our time there. He went to a bilingual school and loved everything from the daily lunches to his school uniform. He also learned enough French for him to make French his chosen second language throughout his later school years.

In 1965 one still had the choice between an ocean crossing and air travel to Europe.

Tom had been sent ahead of us to Paris, so Christopher and I sailed on the Holland America Line's "New Amsterdam." Since the law firm paid for our passage, we went first class, which was quite a change from my earlier crossings. The New Amsterdam was a wonderful ship, great service and friendly to children who had the run of the ship and were allowed to blow the noon whistle every day. I wore long skirts for dinner, met interesting people and ate extremely well.

On the return voyage in November of 1965, Christopher and I again sailed without Tommy who had gone back ahead of us. We sailed on the "United States" which I thought looked like an ugly Hilton Hotel, without charm or elegance.

Our first class cabin was a vast expanse of gray carpet and beige furniture. The service was very basic and the stewards acted put upon. The head dining room steward used to whisper to me "I am sorry Madam, but all the staff are UNION." The food was strictly American, with huge steaks and breast of turkey. The thick cuts of beef that overhung the plates they were served on were especially unappetizing during the rough weather we had for most of the crossing.

Christopher, however, loved having hot dogs, hamburgers and American ice cream. After the thin French milk, he guzzled the rich American version and drank quarts of orange juice. Most of our fellow passengers were American military personnel being rotated back to the States, but I do remember the painter Salvador Dali who walked his pet panther every day on the boat deck.

After we returned from France, Christopher and I lived in Madison with Tom coming on weekends. But the marriage could not be saved. We were divorced in 1968.

I was awarded the house in Madison and Christopher was able to finish his primary education at a small Country Day School. He graduated cum laude and was awarded a scholarship to Choate-Rosemary Hall.

After our divorce, Tom left the law firm and disappeared for a couple of years without paying alimony. Those were very difficult years for me financially. I did all kinds of odd jobs, rented the house in the summer and house-sat for people who needed someone to take care of their house during their summer absence. Eventually, Tom surfaced again in Arizona, but by getting a low-paying job, he was able to have a judge reduce alimony to a bare minimum.

But by carefully managing our resources, especially by renting the house in Madison during the summer months, I was able to take Christopher to Europe one more time on what turned out to be a very successful trip. In 1969 we went back to Henndorf where, together with my sister Christine, her husband and three children, we rented rooms in a private house near Lake Wallersee. Christopher enjoyed his cousins—Gabriela, who was his age, and Gabriela's two brothers who were a couple of years younger. Christine and her husband even took Christopher with them for a two-week stay at a Catholic family retreat near Vienna. Most of the other families there were from Vienna. Christopher had a good time and learned o speak German quite well, albeit with a rather broad Viennese dialect.

The highlight of the summer, however, was a trip through northern Italy that we took with our distant relatives, Fritz Prohaska and his two nephews. They were very knowledgeable about art and music, and great fun to be with. Fritz, a university professor, was about my age; Wolfgang, son of Felix Prohaska the conductor, was curator of 19th century art at the Vienna museum; and his brother Andreas was an aspiring opera singer.

We drove through the Dolomites to Verona, where we saw two operas at the great arena of Verona. Christopher loved every minute of the spectacle on stage, but especially the wine that Wolfi and Andreas let him partake in, directly from the bottle. We were able to see the Villa Valmarana with its Giotto frescoes near Vicenza (a treat as it is open only by special permission) and the great Palladio Villa with the Teatro Olimpico. We went to Padua and saw the Capella degli Scrovegni, again a Giotto masterpiece. All of this was expertly commented on by Wolfgang and, to this day, Christopher remembers what he saw and learned.

We ended up in Venice with more sightseeing, but also a visit to the Lido for Chris to play and cavort in the lukewarm waters of the Adriatic. We ate great food, with Christopher becoming addicted to squid. Fried, pickled, you name it—he loved it!

It was only during the endless visits to churches that he became bored. He sat in a pew and read Time Magazine. As people walked around and spoke in hushed tones as one does in a church, Christopher was heard to exclaim loudly: "Mommy, I am reading, please explain what is for-ni-cation??"

We all had a wonderful trip, and for the first time in years, I felt unencumbered and happy.

Upon returning to the States, I became a travel agent and worked as manager of a Travel Agency in Madison. Christopher graduated cum laude from Choate and went on to Bowdoin College. After graduating from Bowdoin he went to Arizona to spend some time with his father. He eventually went to Arizona State Law School.

The Post Madison Years

Looking back on those years in Madison, I remember only the good things—the pride I took in Christopher's progress and the support of my many friends. I remember the early spring flowers in my garden and the early morning walks on the beach with the water reflecting the rising sun. I remember the joy of discovering Baroque music and focusing on Mozart's piano concertos. I listened to a lot of music then, and still do. Whether it is Gershwin or Vivaldi, music will always lift my spirits.

In 1978 I sold the house in Madison and got a job with the Austrian National Tourist Office in New York.

I got a small one-bedroom apartment on East 87th Street in New York with a good convertible couch in the living room for Christopher to sleep on.

The next 19 years were by far the best years of my life. I was in charge of Ski and Sports Marketing at the Austrian Tourist Office. I had no marketing background, but with a flair for organization, a lot of common sense and a love for mountains, skiing and hiking, I was able to sell Austria with great conviction.

I took members of the ski travel industry on "ski familiarization" trips to Austria. My trips featured the ski resorts I thought would sell well in the U.S. They were meticulously organized, and since I treated my partners in Austria as personal friends—from the people at the tourist offices to ski instructors to hotel owners and their staff—I could always count on their cooperation. The trips I ran became well-known—everyone wanted to go and ski in Austria with Dorli. We all had fun, and I got to ski two or three weeks out of every winter and was paid overtime if we skied on Saturday and Sunday.

I became a sought-after speaker on lecture tours about skiing in Europe, and represented Austria at the famous "Ski Group" shows all over the country.

I finally retired the year I turned 70 and moved to Seattle, where Christopher had become established as a lawyer.

I love Seattle, with its abundance of water and great views of snow-capped mountains and spectacular volcanoes.

I have a small apartment overlooking Lake Washington and count myself very lucky. I live near my son Christopher and his family. He and his wife Ruth have two children, Andrew and Claire. My two grandchildren have become the new focus in my life and I am content.

978-0-595-43276-9
0-595-43276-X

Printed in the United States
91945LV00004B/421-468/A